NEW EDITION

BOOK **1**

by **Robert Lado**

Professor of Linguistics
School of Languages and Linguistics
Georgetown University

in collaboration with

Jerome C. Ford
Bernadette Sheridan, I.H.M.
Annette Silverio-Borges

Regents Publishing Company, Inc.

Illustrations by Bill Kresse

Copyright © 1978 by
Regents Publishing Company, Inc.

Published by
Regents Publishing Company, Inc.
2 Park Avenue
New York, N.Y. 10016

Printed in the United States of America

ISBN 0-88345-328-2
8-85

Table of Contents

Preface i

Unit 1   **Introducing a friend** 1
Affirmative statements 4
Yes/no questions with *is* 6
Sound [i] *ship* 12

Unit 2   **Getting acquainted** 13
Forms of the verb *be* (*am, are, is*) 15
Contractions of the verb *be* (*'m, 's, 're*) 17
Plurals of nouns 21
Yes/no questions with the verb *be* 22
Sound [iy] *sheep* 26

Unit 3   **Identifying a person** 27
Affirmative short answers with *be* 29
Negative statements with *be* 31
Negative short answers with *be* 33
Contrast [i] *ship* and [iy] *sheep* 36

Unit 4   **Greeting a friend** 38
Information questions with *be* 43
The articles *a* and *the* 46
The articles *a* and *an* 49
Articles with singular and plural nouns 50
Modifiers of nouns 52
Sound [z] *zip* 56

Unit 5   **Visiting a friend** 57
Present progressive tense 60
Negative statements in the present progressive 63
Yes/no questions in the present progressive 65
Short answers in the present progressive 66
Information questions in the present progressive 68
Sound [s] *sip* 73

Unit 6   **Answering the phone and taking a message** 74
Requests 76
Polite requests 77
Object pronouns 78
Verbs with two objects 80
The colors 84
Questions about colors 89
Contrast [z] *zip* and [s] *sip* 93

Unit 7   **Talking about occupations** 94
Regular present tense 97
Third person singular of the present tense 100
The days of the week 102
Sound [d] *day* 105

Unit 8   **Ordering dinner at a restaurant** 106
Negative statements in the present tense 108
Yes/no questions in the present tense 110
Short answers in the present tense 114
Sound [ð] *they* 119

Unit 9   **Sightseeing** 120
Demonstrative pronouns 122
Parts of the body 125
Irregular plurals 127
Numbers 1 to 20 128
There is/there are 129
Questions with *there is/there are* 131
Short answers with *there is/there are* 132
The contractions *isn't* and *aren't* 135
Contrast [d] *day* and [ð] *they* 138

Unit 10   **Planning a program** 140
Possessive adjectives 142
Possessive forms of nouns 145
Pronunciation of possessives 148
Subject questions 150
Sound [č] *chin* 155

Key to pronunciation symbols 157
Vocabulary list 159
Index 171

Preface

The second edition of the *Lado English Series* is a complete course in English consisting of six carefully graded levels, with a textbook, workbook, teacher's manual, and cassettes for each level. The central objective of the series is to help students in the complex business of learning to understand, speak, read, and write English. In the new edition, careful attention has been given to the importance of learning to use these four skills for meaningful communication.

The chief innovative feature of the second edition is "contextualization," that is, the placing of all new structures and vocabulary in meaningful contexts, so that the student is always sure of the meaning of the sentences being presented or practiced. New "conversations" are introduced with a background situation which places them in a natural communicative setting. The substitution drills which formerly followed the conversation section have been transformed into "adaptations," which relate structures introduced in the dialogue to other situations in which they may be used. The "practices" are often centered on a context, and are usually accompanied by pictures, which clarify the meaning of each sentence and provide the student with non-verbal cues. In general, the exercises in the new edition are designed to guide the student to a more creative use of the language in activities that closely approximate a normal communicative situation. All this has been achieved while maintaining the advantages of graded, organized learning.

The second edition has retained the same qualities of simplicity of presentation and transparent organization evident in the previous edition. Each unit of the student's text is divided into sections with clear, single-word headings indicating the purpose of the sections: *Conversation, Adaptation, Study, Practice, Speak, Read, Think,* and *Pronounce.*

Each Conversation in the first three books is short, for easier dramatization. It introduces practical topics and useful sentences, and provides a context for the presentation of new material in the unit. A background situation, which can be found in the teacher's manual, describes an appropriate context for the conversation. Intonation lines show the most usual intonation for each sentence, although many other intonations are also possible. These lines represent the four intonation levels of English: low, mid, high, and extra high. The sharp corners used in the previous edition have been replaced with curves, which more accurately represent a change from one level to another. A dot on an intonation line indicates the principal stress in each sentence.

The Adaptation section following each conversation takes up significant parts of the dialogue, usually a question and answer or a statement and comment. The student modifies these sentence pairs with the help of vocabulary cues, thus creating short dialogues which adapt the structures of the conversation to new situations.

The Study sections present grammatical points in simple, easy-to-read frames which help the student visualize each point quickly. A great effort has been made to find the clearest method of presentation for each structure. At the bottom of each frame are recommendations or rules for the use of the grammar point involved.

A Practice section follows each study frame. It consists of exercises which give the student a chance to practice in context the structures just presented. Experience has shown that students master the grammar most quickly when they understand it and use it at the same time. "Contextualization" has resulted in a major reworking of the Practice section. The exercises are made up of sentences which make contextual sense in addition to exemplifying the rule or feature of the study frame. In many cases an entire exercise relates to a single context. In others, responses depend on information supplied by pictures.

The Speak section focuses on using newly learned vocabulary and grammar in a variety of situations. The dialogues in this section are not to be memorized, but are rather to be read aloud and acted out by pairs or groups of students. The dialogues are then gradually modified until students are using the basic outline they provide to express real information about themselves.

The Read section combines the material presented in the unit with material from previous units in interesting reading passages which are to be read silently for meaning. Some new vocabulary is generally included as well. Through the use of these passages, the student's reading skill is developed gradually, moving from a supporting position in Book 1 to a position of major importance in Books 4, 5, and 6.

A Think section appears in every unit beginning with Book 2. It provides an opportunity for the student to use English more freely, and focuses on thought as the natural stimulus for the use of language. The pictures in this section are meant to encourage students to use new structures and vocabulary more creatively, the creative use of language being an essential part of the process of attaining competence in another language.

The Pronounce sections focus on elements of pronunciation which may cause problems both in understanding spoken English and in speaking it. These sections progressively treat all the phonemes of English. Facial diagrams provide a graphic description of the articulation of each sound. These sections also deal with consonant clusters, and particular pronunciation problems due to English spelling, stress, and intonation.

Every workbook after Workbook 1 begins with a Refresher Unit covering the material taught in the preceding level. It consists of a diagnostic test which singles out the points of pronunciation and grammar the students have not yet mastered, a review section which enables the student to selectively review these points, and a second diagnostic test to check whether all the material has been learned. This new unit will provide a useful review not only for those students who have completed the previous course, but also for those who have completed different curricula.

The six Workbooks are designed to complement the learning activities covered in the textbooks. They offer additional exercises to help students master the material in each unit, with the focus on listening, reading, and writing. They also provide conversational activities which can be done in groups.

The Teacher's Manuals have been thoroughly revised and expanded. There is now a separate manual for each textbook. Each page of the manual includes a reduced copy of the corresponding page from the textbook for easy reference. The answers to all the exercises are given together with the reduced page. All the new vocabulary presented in the unit is listed at the beginning of each section. This is followed by a detailed explanation of how to teach the section. Many suggestions for games are also given, so that students can have the chance to practice English in less formal situations. Answers to all workbook exercises can be found in the appendix.

There is a set of Cassettes for each textbook. They give the students the opportunity to listen to native speech, and can be used outside of class to provide extra speaking and listening practice.

It is our hope that the second edition will be even more useful and effective than the first, and we are sure that you will find this edition both appealing and highly functional for the task of teaching your students to communicate in English.

ROBERT LADO
Washington, D.C.

Unit 1

Conversation:
Introducing a friend

Bill

Philip

Linda

Bill: Linda, this is Philip.
Philip is a student.
He's American.
Philip, this is Linda.
Linda is a tourist.
She's English.

Linda, this is Philip.

Philip is a student.

He's American.

Philip, this is Linda.

Linda is a tourist.

She's English.

1

Adaptation

Construct new sentences like the model, using the cues. Construct additional sentences using real names.

1. *Linda, this is Philip.*
   Philip, this is Linda.   Linda   Philip

   Bill, _____ .
   Rosa, _____ .   Bill   Rosa

   Julia, _____ .
   Victor, _____ .   Julia   Victor

   Albert, _____ .
   Carolyn, _____ .   Albert   Carolyn

   Carmen, _____ .
   Toshi, _____ .   Carmen   Toshi

   Oscar, _____ .
   Yoko, _____ .   Oscar   Yoko

2. Philip/student.
   American.

   Philip is a student.
   He's American.

   Bill/salesman.
   American.

   _____ .
   _____ .

Aki/doctor.
Japanese.

_____.
_____.

Albert/tourist.
French.

_____.
_____.

3. Linda/tourist.
English.

Linda is a tourist.
She's English.

Yoko/secretary.
Japanese.

_____.
_____.

Julia/doctor.
Brazilian.

_____.
_____.

Carmen/nurse.
Peruvian.

_____.
_____.

Study 1

Affirmative statements: *Philip is a student.*

Notice the noun phrase and the verb phrase:

This	**is Philip.**
Philip	**is a student.**
He	**'s American.**
This	**is Linda.**
Linda	**is English.**
She	**'s a tourist.**

He's is the contraction of **he is.**
She's is the contraction of **she is.**
Use the contractions in conversation.

Practice

Construct new sentences like the model, using the cues. Construct additional sentences using real or invented names and information.

Linda
tourist
English

This is Linda.
She's a tourist.
She's English.

ENGLAND

Linda

Bill
salesman
American

This is Bill.
He's a salesman.
He's American.

Bill

UNITED STATES

4

Victor
doctor
Colombian

Victor

COLOMBIA

Rosa
saleswoman
Italian

ITALY

Rosa

Oscar
teacher
Puerto Rican

Oscar

PUERTO RICO

Monique
scientist
French

FRANCE

Monique

Manuel
mechanic
Venezuelan

Manuel

VENEZUELA

Toshi
tourist
Japanese

JAPAN

Toshi

Carolyn
teacher
American

Carolyn

UNITED
STATES

Study 2

Yes/no questions with **is**: *Is Philip in class?*

Notice the position of **is** in the questions:

Philip   **is**   in class.

Is	Philip	in class?
Is	Linda	in England?
Is	she	sick?
Is	this	Philip?
Is	Philip	a tourist?
Is	he	American?
Is	this	Linda?
Is	she	a student?
Is	she	English?

Put **is** in the first position in the questions.

Practice

1. Ask and answer the following questions. Notice the contrast in the word pairs.

Is Philip *tall?*

No. He's *short.*

Bill   Philip

Is Linda *sad?*
No. She's *happy.*   Linda   Jane

Is Mary *present?*
No. She's *absent.*   Lynn   Mary

Is Victor *sick?*
No. He's *fine.*   Victor   John

Is Francis *old?*
No. He's *young.*   Louise   Francis

Is Francis *right?*
No. He's *wrong.*   Rose   Francis

2. Construct yes/no questions using the cues. Answer the questions
   according to the pictures.

Philip?

in class?

Philip

Is this Philip?
Yes. This is Philip.
Is he in class?
Yes. He's in class.

Bill?

old?

Francis

Is this Bill?
No. This is Francis.
Is he old?
No. He's young.

Alice?

sick?

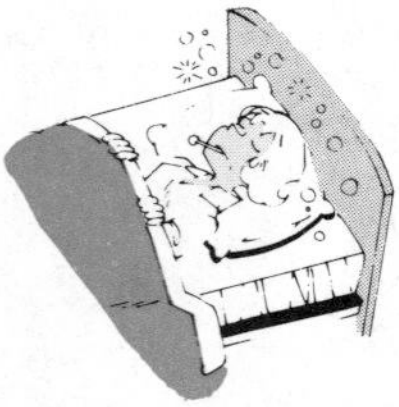

Alice

_____ ?

___ . _____ .

_____ ?

___ . _____ .

Lynn?

absent?

Lynn

_____ ?

___ . _____ .

_____ ?

___ . _____ .

Christine?

tall?

Christine

_____ ?

___ . _____ .

_____ ?

___ . _____ .

Toshi?

sad?

Toshi

_____ ?

___ . _____ .

_____ ?

___ . _____ .

Speak

1. Ask and answer yes/no questions based on the map.

Is Philip in Bolivia?
▶ *No. He's in the United States.*

Is Linda in the United States?
▶ *Yes. She's in New York.*

Is Carmen in Caracas?
▶ *No. She's in Lima.*

9

Carolyn Jackson

Philip

Mary Lynn Donald Carlos

Philip Ann

2. Ask and answer yes/no questions based on the picture of the math class.

Is Carolyn Jackson a doctor?
▶ *No. She's a teacher.*
Is Lynn in class?
▶ *Yes. She's in class.*
Is Mary present?
▶

Is Carlos sick?
▶
Is Carlos a tourist?
▶

Is Donald absent?
▶
Is Donald sad?
▶
Is Ann in class?
▶
Is Ann a teacher?
▶
Is Philip late?
▶

Read

Pictures in an album

Donald: Is this Robert?
 Philip: No. This is Paul.
He's a student in Boston.
Robert is a mechanic in New York City.

Donald: Is this a museum?
 Philip: No. This is a hospital.
Victor is a doctor in this hospital.

Donald: Is this Linda Wilson?
 Philip: No. This is Alice Hill.
She's a nurse in New York City.
She's American.

Donald: Is this Peru?
 Philip: Yes. This is Lima.
Carmen is a nurse in Lima.

Answer the questions.

1. Is Paul a student or a mechanic?
2. Is he in New York City?
3. Is Victor in a museum or a hospital?
4. Is Alice Hill American?
5. Is Carmen in Chile?

11

Pronounce

ship [i]	front, open, lax
	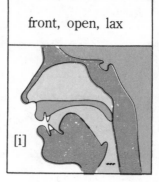 [i]

this
Victor
Linda
Philip
Vincent
Alice
English
Bill
is

Is this a ship?
Yes. This is a ship.

Is this Bill?
No. This is Philip.

 Philip

Is this Linda?
No. This is Alice.

 Alice

Unit 2

Conversation: Getting acquainted

Linda Wilson

Bill and Philip Sullivan

Linda: Are you and Bill friends?
Philip: No. We're brothers.
Linda: Brothers? He's tall, and you're short!
Philip: My father is short.
Linda: Is your mother short?
Philip: No. She's tall.

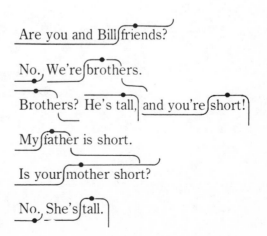

13

Adaptation

Construct new sentences like the model, using the cue words. Construct additional sentences using real or invented names and information.

1. Bill/friends?   *Are you and Bill friends?*
   brothers.   *No. We're brothers.*

   Alice/sisters?   _____?
   cousins.   _____ . _____.

   Linda/brother and sister? _____?
   friends.   _____ . _____.

   Oscar/mechanics?   _____?
   teachers.   _____ . _____.

   Julia/nurses?   _____?
   doctors.   _____ . _____.

2. tall, short.   *He's tall, and you're short.*
   young, old.   _____.
   American, English.   _____.
   sad, happy.   _____.
   a teacher, a saleswoman. _____.

3. mother/short?   *Is your mother short?*
   tall.   *No. She's tall.*

   father/a teacher?   _____?
   doctor.   _____ . _____.

   mother/a doctor?   _____?
   scientist.   _____ . _____.

14

sister/sick? _____?

fine. _____ . _____ .

brother/present? _____?

absent. _____ . _____ .

father/old? _____?

young. _____ . _____ .

Study 1

Forms of the verb **be (am, are, is):** *My father is short.*

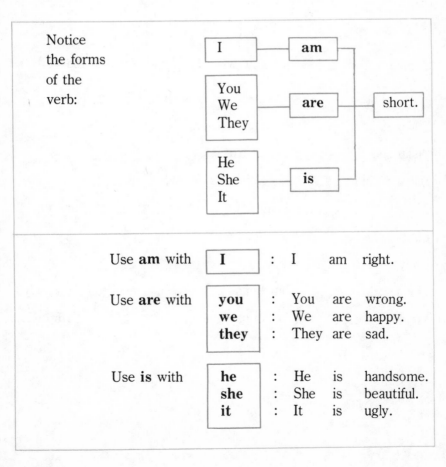

Notice the forms of the verb:

I	—	am
You We They	—	are	— short.
He She It	—	is

Use **am** with **I** : I am right.

Use **are** with **you** : You are wrong.
  we : We are happy.
  they : They are sad.

Use **is** with **he** : He is handsome.
  she : She is beautiful.
  it : It is ugly.

15

Are is used with
the singular
and plural
of **you:**

Singular:

You **are** a tourist.

Plural:

You **are** tourists.

Practice

Complete the sentences below with the proper form of the verb **be.**

Philip ____*is*____ short.

Philip and Bill ____*are*____ brothers.

Bill and Linda _____ friends.   We _____ in class.

Bill _____ handsome.   I _____ present.

Linda _____ beautiful.   You _____ right.

They _____ happy.   I _____ wrong.

Linda _____ from London.   You _____ happy.

London _____ beautiful.   We _____ friends.

Study 2

Contractions of the verb **be** (**'m, 's, 're**): *He's tall, and you're short!*

Notice the contracted forms of the verb **be:**

Singular:

I am **I'm**	short.
You are **You're**	short.
He is **He's**	tall.
She is **She's**	tall.
It is **It's**	high.

Plural:

We are **We're**	happy.
You are **You're**	sad.
They are **They're**	sick.

'm
is the contraction of **am.**
's
is the contraction of **is.**
're
is the contraction of **are.**

Use the contractions in conversation.

Practice

1. Answer the question according to the picture. Use the correct form of **be** and the appropriate personal pronoun.

ENGLAND

Are you American?
▶ *No. I'm English.*

Is he Colombian?
▶ *Yes. He's Colombian.*

COLOMBIA

Are they absent?
▶

Are we in Washington?
▶

WASHINGTON

Is she sad?
▶

Am I sick?
▶

Are you tourists?
▶

Are you happy?
▶

18

2. Answer with **it**.

Is New York in Canada?
▶ *No. It's in the United States.*

Is Mexico City in the United States?
▶ *No. It's in Mexico.*

Is Miami in Puerto Rico?
▶

Is Havana in Canada?
▶

Is San Francisco in Cuba?
▶

Is Berlin in Italy?
▶

Is Dublin in Portugal?
▶

Is Madrid in France?
▶

Is Rome in England?
▶

Continue with other cities on the map or with another map.

3. Answer the question according to the picture. Use **it**.

Is this Ann?
▶ *No. It's Lynn.*

Lynn

Is this Roy?
▶ *Yes. It's Roy.*

Roy

Is this a saleswoman?
▶

Is this a man?
▶

Is this Portugal?
▶

PUERTO RICO

Is this a woman?
▶

Is this a dog?
▶

Study 3

Plurals of nouns: *We're brothers.*

Notice the formation of plurals with different nouns:

I'm	a lawyer.	► We're lawyers.
You're	a mechanic.	► You're mechanics.
He's	a cook.	► They're cooks.
She's	a nurse.	► They're nurses.
It's	a city.	► They're cities.
It's	a watch.	► They're watches.

Omit **a** in the plural.

21

Practice

Change to the plural.

He's a doctor.
▶ *They're doctors.*

It's a dog.
▶

It's a class.
▶

I'm a tourist.
▶ *We're tourists.*

He's a friend.
▶

You're a teacher.
▶

It's a school.
▶ *They're schools.*

It's a city.
▶

He's a cook.
▶

I'm a student.
▶

You're a secretary.
▶

It's a watch.
▶

She's a nurse.
▶

I'm a lawyer.
▶

Study 4

Yes/no questions with the verb **be:** *Are you friends?*

Notice the position of the verb in the questions:

Philip **is** short.

Is Philip short?

Linda and Bill **are** friends.

Are Linda and Bill friends?

Am I right?   No. You **are** wrong.

Are you sick?   Yes. I **am** sick.

Is she here?   Yes. She **is** here.

Is math difficult?   No. It **is** easy.

Are we friends?   Yes. We **are** friends.

Are you cousins?   No. We **are** brothers.

Are they happy?   No. They **are** sad.

Place the verb **am, are,** or **is** in the first position in the questions.

Practice

Ask a question for each picture below, using the words given. Answer the questions.

Linda/a tourist?

Is Linda a tourist?
Yes. She's a tourist.

you/sick?

Are you sick?
No. I'm fine.

Carmen/nurse?

_____?
_____.

Victor and Julia/
doctors?

_____?
_____.

Linda and Toshi/
tourists?

_____?
_____.

Toshi/Japanese?

_____?
_____.

Francis/right?

2+2=7

_____?
_____.

I/right?

2+2=4

_____?
_____.

Speak

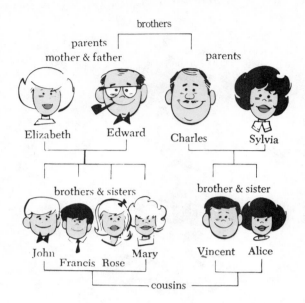

Linda: Are Edward and Charles brothers or cousins?
  Bill: They're brothers.
Linda: Are Vincent and Alice brother and sister?
  Bill: Yes. They're brother and sister.
Linda: Are John and Francis cousins?
  Bill: No. They're brothers.
Linda: Are Mary and Alice sisters or cousins?
  Bill: _____ .
Linda: Are Rose and Mary sisters?
  Bill: _____ .
Linda: Are Sylvia and Charles parents?
  Bill: _____ .

Continue with other questions about the picture.

Read

My family in New York

This is my family. We are in New York now. My father is short, and my mother is tall. He is a mechanic. She is a nurse. They are happy. My sister and I are short. My cousin is tall. My parents are old, and we are young. My sister is a travel agent. She is happy. My cousin is a tourist. She is very happy. I am a student. I am unhappy. My father is Venezuelan, and my mother is Colombian. My cousin is Colombian, but my sister and I are American.

Answer the questions:

1. Are they in Colombia or New York?
2. Is the mother tall or short?
3. Are the parents happy or sad?
4. Is the cousin a tourist or a travel agent?
5. Are the mother and father Venezuelan or Colombian?

Pronounce

sheep [iy]

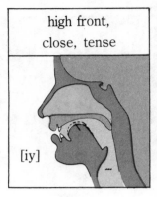

high front,
close, tense

[iy]

he
Edith
Eugene
s**he**
Peter
Kathl**ee**n
Eve
t**ea**cher
Christine

Christine, this is Peter.

Is Peter a teacher?
Yes. He's a teacher.

Is Eve a teacher?
Yes. She's a teacher.

Is this a sheep?
Yes. It's a sheep.

Unit 3

Conversation: Identifying a person

Jack Newman

Barbara Stern

Jack: Are you Linda Wilson?
Barbara: No, I'm not. I'm Barbara Stern.
Jack: Are you and Linda friends?
Barbara: Yes, we are.
Jack: Is she here today?
Barbara: No, she's not. She's sick.

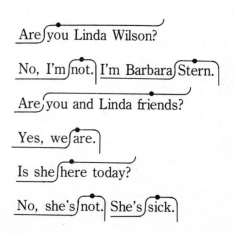

27

Adaptation

1. you Linda Wilson? *Are you Linda Wilson?*
   Barbara Stern. *No, I'm not. I'm Barbara Stern.*
   she here today? *Is she here today?*
   sick. *No, she's not. She's sick.*

   he Philip Sullivan? _____?
   Jack Newman. _____ . _____.
   he French? _____?
   American. _____ . _____.

   you a tourist? _____?
   a saleswoman. _____ . _____.
   you French? _____?
   Italian. _____ . _____.

   she American? _____?
   Brazilian. _____ . _____.
   she sick? _____?
   fine. _____ . _____.

2. you and Linda friends? *Are you and Linda friends?*
   Yes, *Yes, we are.*

   you and Bill cousins? _____?
   Yes, _____.

   Philip and Bill brothers? _____?
   Yes, _____.

   Philip and Alice students? _____?
   Yes, _____.

   Alice and I cousins? _____?
   Yes, _____.

Study 1

Affirmative short answers with **be**: *Yes, we are.*

Notice the omission of the noun or adjective in the short answers:

Are you hungry?	**Yes, I am.**
Am I friendly?	**Yes, you are.**
Is Bill a salesman?	**Yes, he is.**
Is Linda sick?	**Yes, she is.**
Is London nice?	**Yes, it is.**
Are you and Linda thirsty?	**Yes, we are.**
Are Paul and I handsome?	**Yes, you are.**
Are Philip and Ann friends?	**Yes, they are.**

Short answers with **be** end with **am, are,** or **is.**

No contractions are used in short answers beginning with **yes.**

Practice

1. Answer with affirmative short answers: **he is, she is, it is,** and **they are.**

Is Barbara friendly?
▶ *Yes, she is.*

Are Barbara and Jack happy?
▶ *Yes, they are.*

Jack   Barbara

Is Barbara hungry?
▶

Are Barbara and Jack thirsty?
▶

Is math difficult?
▶

Is Philip unhappy?
▶

Philip

Are Bill and Christine tall?
▶

Is Christine happy?
▶

Christine   Bill

Is San Francisco in the United States?
▶

Is it beautiful?
▶

San Francisco

2. Construct yes/no questions using the words below, and respond with the affirmative answers: **I am, you are,** and **we are.**

you/hungry?   *Are you hungry?*
                               Yes, I am.

you and Jack/friends?   *Are you and Jack friends?*
                               Yes, we are.

you/thirsty? _____?

_____.

you/tourists? _____?

_____.

I/friendly? _____?

_____.

you and I/happy? _____?

_____.

you and Philip/students? _____?

_____.

I/tall? _____?

_____.

you/a salesman? _____?

_____.

I/handsome? _____?

_____.

Study 2

Negative statements with **be:** *I'm not Linda Wilson.*

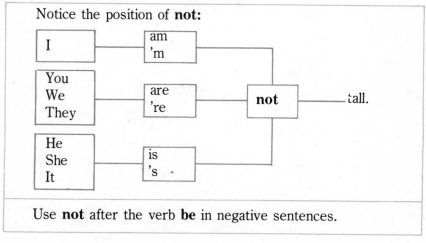

Use **not** after the verb **be** in negative sentences.

31

Practice

Answer with negative or affirmative statements with **be.** Use the pictures for cues when necessary.

Is London in the United States?
▶ *No. It's not in the United States.*

London

Are you from London?
▶ *Yes. I'm from London.*

Are you and Toshi students?
▶ *No. We're not students.*

Toshi   Linda

Am I short?
▶

Ramón

Is Ramón in Costa Rica?
▶

MEXICO

Is Linda sick?
▶

Linda

Are Frank and Carlos in school?

▶

Are you Linda Wilson?

▶

Barbara Stern

Are Robert and I teachers?

▶

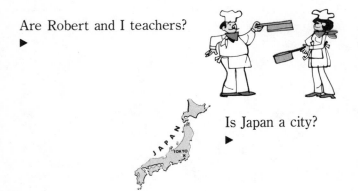

Is Japan a city?

▶

Study 3

Negative short answers with **be:** *No, I'm not.*

Notice the position of **not:**

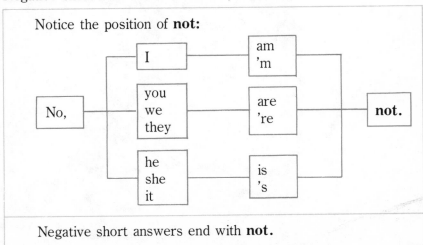

No,	I	am / 'm	
	you / we / they	are / 're	**not.**
	he / she / it	is / 's	

Negative short answers end with **not.**

Practice

Answer the following questions with negative short answers.

Is London in the United States? *No, it's not.*

Is Linda in London? *No, she's not.*

Are Barbara and Linda sisters? *No, they're not.*

Are you and Barbara friends? _____ .

Is Barbara from Japan? _____ .

Is English difficult? _____ .

Is Japanese easy? _____ .

Am I absent today? _____ .

Are we at a party now? _____ .

Are you sick today? _____ .

Are you and I cousins? _____ .

Are Jack and Barbara cousins? _____ .

Speak

Margaret, John, and David are in Washington.

Margaret: Good morning, John.

John: Hello, Margaret.

Margaret, this is David. He's from Chicago.

Margaret: Hello, David.

Are you a student?

David: No, I'm not. I'm a lawyer. I'm a tourist in Washington.

Are you a student?

Margaret: Yes, I am.

David: Are you from Washington?

Margaret: No, I'm not. I'm from San Francisco.

David: Is San Francisco ugly?

Margaret: No, it's not! It's beautiful!

Are you and John friends?

David: Yes, we are.

Margaret: Is he from Chicago?

David: No, he's not. He's from Miami.

Read

Joseph and Rose are brother and sister. They are tourists. He is in Berlin. She is in Madrid. Berlin and Madrid are not countries. They are cities. Berlin is in Germany. Madrid is in Spain. Germany and Spain are countries. They are in Europe. Europe is big. It is interesting.

Answer the questions.

1. Are Joseph and Rose cousins?
2. Is Rose in Madrid?
3. Are Madrid and Berlin cities?
4. Are they in the United States?
5. Is Spain a country?

Michael and Kathleen are not brother and sister. They are friends. He is from Chicago. She is from Dublin. Michael is a pilot. He is tall and handsome. He is in Dublin now. Kathleen is a travel agent. She is not sad. She is very happy.

Answer the questions.

1. Are Kathleen and Michael brother and sister?
2. Is Michael from Chicago?
3. Is Kathleen from Chicago?
4. Is Michael tall and handsome?
5. Is Kathleen sad?

Pronounce

Contrast [i] and [iy].

ship [i]	sheep [iy]

ship
sick
this
sister
it
is

sheep
she
he
Greek
Eve
teacher

Is this Peter?
No. It's Nick.

Is Nick English?
No. He's Greek.

GREECE

Is Bill a teacher?
No, he's not.
Is he sick?
Yes, he is.

Is this ship English?
Yes. This ship is English.

Unit 4

Conversation:
Greeting a friend

Alice Hill

Helen Newman

Alice: Hello, Mrs. Newman. How are you?
Mrs. Newman: I'm fine, thank you.
Alice: Where's Jack?
Mrs. Newman: He's home.
Alice: How is he?
Mrs. Newman: He's sick. He's in bed.

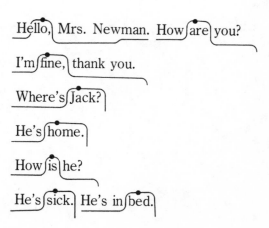

Adaptation

1.

Mrs. Newman

Hello, Mrs. Newman. How are you?
I'm fine, thank you.

Alice

_____ . _____ ?

_____ .

Toshi

_____ . _____ ?

_____ .

Linda

_____ . _____ ?

_____ .

Bill

_____ . _____ ?

_____ .

2.

Jack

Where's Jack?
He's home.

in

Linda

New York City

_____ ?
_____ .

in

Philip

_____ ?
_____ .

in

Carolyn

_____ ?
_____ .

 in

Ramón   MEXICO

_____ ?
_____ .

40

3.  Jack?

How's Jack?
He's sick. He's in bed.

 Michael and Kathleen?

Dublin

How are Michael and Kathleen?
They're fine. They're in Dublin.

 Ann?

_____ ?
_____ . _____ .

41

  Albert and Linda?

_____ ?

_____ . _____ .

 Philip?

_____ ?

_____ . _____ .

 Joseph and Rose?

 EUROPE

_____ ?

_____ . _____ .

Study 1

Information questions with **be**: *How is he?*

Notice the question words **who, what, where,** and **how:**

Is he **Mr. Newman?** No.

Who is he?

Is he **a doctor?** No.

What is he?

Is he **in China?** No.

Where is he?

Is he **sick?** No.

How is he?

Use the appropriate question word in the first position.

Use **who** for identification.

Who? ▶ Mr. Newman
Mrs. Newman

Use **where** for location.

Where? ▶ in Paris

in class

in Spain

Use **what** for classification.

What? ▶ a horse

a man

a nurse

Use **how** for quality or state.

How? ▶ sick

well

fine

Practice

1. Give the information question with **what**, **where**, or **how**, and answer it according to the picture.

Is Mr. Collins a doctor? No, he's not.
▶ *What is he? He's a lawyer.*

Are they sick? No, they're not.
▶ *How are they? They're fine.*

44

Are you in California? No, we're not.
▶ *Where are you? We're in Washington.*

WASHINGTON

Is Donald home? No, he's not.
▶

Is Boston a country? No, it's not.
▶

Are you sick? No, I'm not.
▶

Is Lisbon in Spain? No, it's not.
▶

Is Miss Jackson well? No, she's not.
▶

Are Japan and India cities? No, they're not.
▶

Is London in France? No, it's not.
▶

2. Give the information question for each sentence.

John and Mary are not *in Berlin.*
▶ *Where are John and Mary?*
I am not *sick.*
▶ *How are you?*
He is not *a lawyer.*
▶
I am not *fine.*
▶

45

You are not *American*.
▶

Sylvia and Elizabeth are not *in New York*.
▶

We are not *well*.
▶

Paul Collins is not *in Bonn*.
▶

Barbara and Linda are not *cousins*.
▶

Lima is not *in Bolivia*.
▶

Study 2

The articles **a** and **the**: *The man is tall.*

Notice the use of **a** and **the**:

This is **a book**.
(The object is classified:
It's a book, not a boy.)

The book is small.
(The book is identified.)

A boy and **a man** are
on a bus.

The boy is short.
The man is tall.

The moon is in **the sky.**
(Unique: one moon, one sky)

Use **a** to indicate "classified, categorized."
Use **the** to indicate "identified, specified, unique."

46

Practice

1. Answer the questions according to the pictures.

What is she?
► *She's a doctor.*

What is this?
► *It's a hospital.*

What is this?
►

What is he?
►

What is she?
►

What is this?
►

What is she?
▶

What is he?
▶

2. Make sentences about each picture using the article **the.**

A woman and a boy are in class.
▶ *The boy is a student.*
▶ *The woman is a teacher.*

A pilot and a travel agent are in Dublin.
▶ *The pilot is handsome.*
▶ *The travel agent is beautiful.*

A brother and a sister are in Europe.
▶
▶

A man and a woman are in the room.
▶
▶

48

A man and a woman are in the office.
▶
▶

We are in a city and in a country.
▶
▶

Caracas   VENEZUELA

Study 3

The articles **a** and **an:** *It's a book. It's an apple.*

Notice the sound after **a** and **an:**

It's **a** banana.

It's **a** cat.

It's **an** eye.

It's **an** apple.

Use **a** before consonants.
Use **an** before vowels.

Practice

Answer the question **What is it?** for each of the pictures.

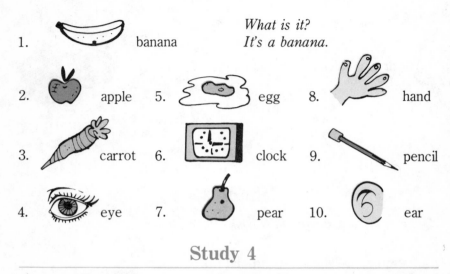

1. banana

What is it?
It's a banana.

2. apple 5. egg 8. hand

3. carrot 6. clock 9. pencil

4. eye 7. pear 10. ear

Study 4

Articles with singular and plural nouns: *He's a pilot. The boys are students.*

Notice the articles **a, an,** and **the** with singular and plural nouns:

a, an:

He's **a tourist.**

They're **tourists.**

It's **an apple.**

They're **apples.**

50

the:

The **student** is intelligent.

The **students** are intelligent.

The **apple** is delicious.

The **apples** are delicious.

Use **a** and **an** with singular nouns only.
Use **the** with singular and plural nouns.

Practice

Change to the plural.

He's a lawyer.
▶ *They're lawyers.*

The lawyer is intelligent.
▶ *The lawyers are intelligent.*

I'm happy.
▶ *We're happy.*

It's a school.
▶

The class is big.
▶

The student is tall.
▶

She's a friend.
▶

The girl is beautiful.
▶

I'm a nurse.
▶

It's a hospital.
▶

The hospital is big.
▶

Study 5

Modifiers of nouns: *He's a good doctor.*

Notice the position of the modifiers **good, young, art,** and **night:**

The doctor is good.	▶ He's a	**good**	doctor.
The dresses are short.	▶ They're	**short**	dresses.
The book is on art.	▶ It's an	**art**	book.
The classes are at night.	▶ They're	**night**	classes.

Modifiers precede the nouns they modify.

Practice

1. Answer the questions with **yes,** forming sentences with modified nouns.

   Is the story interesting?
   ▶ *Yes. It's an interesting story.*

   Are the problems easy?
   ▶ *Yes. They're easy problems.*

   Is the city big?
   ▶

Is the man tall?

▶

Is the song nice?

▶

Is the dinner excellent?

▶

Is the country beautiful?

▶

Are the students intelligent?

▶

Are the exercises difficult?

▶

Are the apples delicious?

▶

Are the cities old?

▶

2. Complete the sentence with the same noun, but put the modifier before the noun.

A museum of art is *an art museum.*
A book on history is *a history book.*
A class in geography is *a geography class.*
A teacher of chemistry is _____ .
A book on science is _____ .
A job at night is _____ .
A class in literature is _____ .
A book on philosophy is _____ .
A lesson in English is _____ .
A worker in a factory is _____ .
A worker in an office is _____ .
A bed in a hospital is _____ . 53

Speak

Frank and Carlos are playing a guessing game.

1. **Frank:** What is it?
   Carlos: It's a city.
   Frank: Where is it?
   Carlos: It's in Europe.
   Frank: Is it big?
   Carlos: Yes, it is.
   Frank: Is it a capital?
   Carlos: Yes, it is.
   Frank: Is it ugly?
   Carlos: No, it's not.
   Frank: Is it in France?
   Carlos: Yes, it is.
   Frank: Is it Paris?
   Carlos: Yes, it is.

2. **Carlos:** What is it?
   Frank: It's a man.
   Carlos: Where is he?
   Frank: He's in the hospital.
   Carlos: Is he sick?
   Frank: No, he's not.
   Carlos: Is he fine?
   Frank: Yes, he is.
   Carlos: Is he a doctor?
   Frank: Yes, he is.
   Carlos: Is he Dr. Graham?
   Frank: Yes, he is.

Answer the questions.

1. What is Paris?
2. Where is it?
3. Is it a capital?
4. Is it ugly?

Answer the questions.

1. Is Dr. Graham sick?
2. How is he?
3. Where is he?
4. What is he?

Read

Susan   Edward   Martha

Edward: Hi, Susan. Hi, Martha. How are you?
Susan: We're fine, thanks. How are you?
Edward: Fine, thank you.
Martha: Where is Henry? He's not in the office.
Edward: He's in Boston.
Martha: Oh! Is he from Boston?
Edward: No, he's not. He's from Washington.
He's a tourist in Boston.

Edward: Are you and Jack Newman friends?
Susan: Yes, we are.
Edward: How is Jack?
Susan: He's fine.
Martha: Is he an engineer?
Susan: No, he's not.
Martha: What is he?
Susan: He's a computer programmer.

Answer the questions.

1. How are Susan and Martha?
2. Where is Henry?
3. Is Henry from Boston?
4. Are Susan and Jack friends?
5. What is Jack?

Pronounce

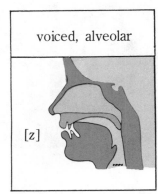

is
please
doctors
he's
Rose
nurses
memorize
easy
busy

Is James in Brazil?
No. He's in Lisbon.

Please tell Elizabeth:
Rose is busy.

Are Charles and Rose doctors?
No. They're nurses.

Unit 5

Conversation:
Visiting a friend

Helen Newman

George Taylor

Sandra Taylor

Helen: Is Sandra home?
George: Yes, she is.
Helen: What is she doing?
George: She's reading.
Helen: Where is she reading?
George: In the living room.

Is Sandra home?

Yes, she is.

What is she doing?

She's reading.

Where is she reading?

In the living room.

57

Adaptation

1. she?
   reading.

What is she doing?
She's reading.

he?
singing.

_____ ?

_____ .

I?
writing.

_____ ?

_____ .

they?
watching
television.

_____ ?

_____ .

58

2. she/reading?
   living room.

Where is she reading?
In the living room.

he/eating?
kitchen.

_____?
_____.

they/talking?
bedroom.

_____?
_____.

Philip/studying?
library.

_____?
_____.

they/working?
office.

_____?
_____.

Study 1

Present progressive tense: *She's reading.*

Notice the verb **be (am, are, is)** and the **-ing** form of the main verb:

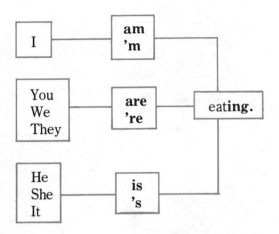

Use the appropriate form of the verb **be (am, are, is)** and the **-ing** form of the main verb **(eating).**

Use the contractions in conversation: **I'm, you're, we're, they're, he's, she's, it's.**

Use the present progressive tense for an activity in progress at the present time:

> I'm thinking **right now.**
> You're reading fast **today.**
> They're talking **now.**
> He's going to school **this year.**

Some verbs, such as **like, want,** and **know,** are not generally used in the present progressive. See the examples in the frame at the top of p. 71.

Practice

1. Answer the questions according to the pictures.

What are you doing now?
I'm studying.

What are they doing?
They're playing the guitar.

What are you doing?
We _____ .

What is she doing?
She _____ .

What am I doing?
You _____ .

What is he doing?
He _____ .

What is it doing?
It _____ .

What are they doing?
They _____ .

2. Answer according to the pictures.

What are you doing,
listening or talking?
▶ *I'm listening.*

What is Helen doing,
sleeping or working?
▶ *She's sleeping.*

What is George doing,
laughing or crying?
▶

What is Sandra doing,
reading or writing?
▶

What is he writing,
a letter or a story?
▶

What are they reading,
a book or a newspaper?
▶

What are they doing,
singing or playing the guitar?
▶

What am I playing,
the guitar or the piano?
▶

What are you doing,
eating or drinking?
▶

Study 2

Negative statements in the present progressive: *I'm not eating.*

Notice the placement of **not:**

I'm	**not**	sleeping.
He's	**not**	singing.
You're	**not**	working.

Place **not** after the verb **be (am, are, is.)**

Practice

Describe the pictures using the word cues.

work

I'm not working.
I'm drinking coffee.

write

She's not writing.
She's reading.

laugh

We're _____ .

_____ .

sleep

It's _____ .

_____ .

play the guitar

He's _____ .

_____ .

dance

They're _____ .

_____ .

listen to the radio   work

I'm _____ .   You're _____ .

_____ .   _____ .

Study 3

Yes/no questions in the present progressive: *Is she reading in the living room?*

Notice the word order in the questions:

	You **are**	eating a banana.
Are	you	eating a banana?
Is	she	eating a pear?
Am	I	eating a carrot?

For questions in the present progressive, use the word order for questions with the verb **be (am, are, is)**. See p. 22.

Practice

Give the yes/no question for the following answer.

Am I singing a nice song?   No.   You're not singing a nice song.
Is she asking a question?   Yes.   She's asking a question.

_____ ?   Yes.   He's reading an art book.
_____ ?   No.   The people are not dancing.
_____ ?   Yes.   We're going now.

65

_____?	Yes. They're listening to the radio.
_____?	No. You're not working today.
_____?	Yes. He's sleeping now.
_____?	Yes. I'm crying.
_____?	No. We're not drinking coffee.

Study 4

Short answers in the present progressive: *Yes, she is.*

Notice	Are you Helen Newman?	**Yes, I am.**
the short	Are you working?	**No, I'm not.**
answers:	Is Sandra home?	**Yes, she is.**
	Is she sleeping?	**No, she's not.**
	Am I a good singer?	**No, you're not.**
	Am I singing a nice song?	**Yes, you are.**

Short answers with the present progressive are the same as short answers with the verb **be.** See p. 29 and p. 33.

Practice

Give short answers with **yes** or **no** according to the pictures.

Is Linda speaking English?
▶ *Yes, she is.*

Are they dancing?
▶ *No, they're not.*

Are you playing tennis?
▶

Are you laughing?
▶

Is she thinking in Spanish?
▶

Is Alice working?
▶

Is the horse sleeping?
▶

Are they reading the
newspaper?
▶

Is he working?
▶

Is she asking a question?
▶

Study 5

Information questions in the present progressive: *What are you reading?*

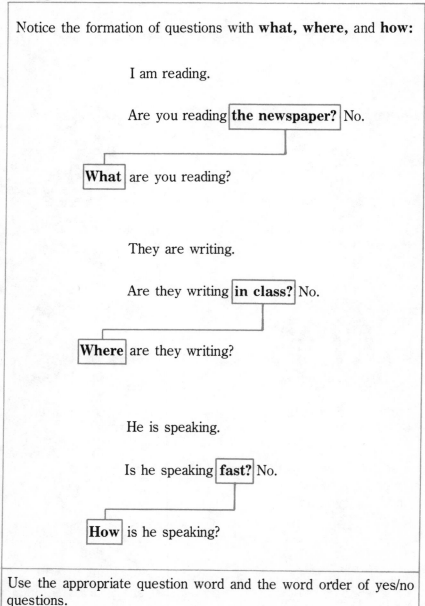

Notice the formation of questions with **what, where,** and **how:**

I am reading.

Are you reading | the newspaper? | No.

What | are you reading?

They are writing.

Are they writing | in class? | No.

Where | are they writing?

He is speaking.

Is he speaking | fast? | No.

How | is he speaking?

Use the appropriate question word and the word order of yes/no questions.

Notice the use of the question word **how:**

How is he speaking?	He's speaking **clearly.**
How am I singing?	You're singing **well.**
How are we going there?	We're going there **by bus.**

To answer a question with **how,** use a phrase with **by (by bus, by car, by taxi),** or use an adverb. Some adverbs are short: **hard, fast, well.** Most adverbs are made by adding **-ly** to adjectives:

clear ▸ **clearly**
quick ▸ **quickly**
slow ▸ **slowly**

Practice

Ask information questions about the pictures with **what, where,** or **how.** Answer the questions.

you doing, listening or speaking?
▸ *What are you doing, listening or speaking?*
▸ *I'm speaking.*
you speaking, clearly or fast?
▸ *How are you speaking, clearly or fast?*
▸ *I'm speaking clearly.*

he doing, reading or writing?
▸
▸
he reading, astronomy or history?
▸
▸

69

they doing, dancing or talking?
▶
▶
they dancing, slowly or fast?
▶
▶

she doing, singing or laughing?
▶
▶
she singing, in a theater or in a club?
▶
▶

you doing, eating or drinking?
▶
▶
you drinking, milk or coffee?
▶
▶

he doing, sleeping or studying?
▶
▶
he studying, in the kitchen or in the bedroom?
▶
▶

I going, to Los Angeles or to San Francisco?
▶
▶
I going, by bus or by car?
▶
▶

Do not use the progressive form with **like, be, see, want, know,** or **need.**

> I **like** apples.
> I **am** very happy.
> I **see** the little boy.
> I **want** the newspaper.
> I **know** Henry.
> I **need** a pencil.

Speak

1. **Carolyn:** Is Philip in school?
   Carlos: Yes. He's in the library.
   Carolyn: What is he doing?
   Carlos: He's studying history.

2.   **Bill:** Where is Alice?
   Mrs. Hill: She's in the living room.
        Bill: What is she doing?
   Mrs. Hill: She's watching television.

3. **Richard:** Where are you going?
   Susan: I'm going to Chicago.
   Richard: How are you going?
   Susan: I'm going by bus.
   Richard: Where are you staying?
   Susan: I'm staying at a motel.

Read

The Taylor family at home

It is eight o'clock. The Taylor family is home. Mr. and Mrs. Taylor are in the kitchen. Mrs. Taylor is washing the dishes and Mr. Taylor is cleaning the table. Donald Taylor is in the bedroom. He is writing a science report and he is working hard. Janice Taylor is playing the piano in the living room. She is practicing a very difficult piece. Dennis Taylor is in the basement with a friend, Carol. They are playing cards and watching television. It's an interesting television show. They are having a good time. The Taylor family is always busy.

Answer the questions.

1. Where is the Taylor family?
2. What are Mr. and Mrs. Taylor doing?
3. What is Donald writing?
4. Who is playing the piano?
5. Is she practicing an easy piece?
6. What are Dennis and Carol doing?
7. How is the television show?
8. Are they having a good time?

Pronounce

sip [s]	voiceless, alveolar
	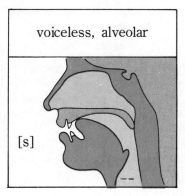

sing
sad
song
Alice
yes
fast
stop
sip
soup

Alice is singing a sad song.
Stop singing that song, Alice!

Vincent is sipping the soup fast.
Stop sipping the soup so fast, Vincent!

Unit 6

Conversation:
Answering the phone
and taking a message

Sandra: Hello?
Richard: Hello. Is Donald there?
Sandra: I'm sorry. He's busy.
Richard: Please give him a message.
Sandra: Excuse me. Wait a minute.
(To George) George. Give me a pencil, please.
(George gives Sandra a pencil.)
O.K. What's the message?
Richard: The game is tonight.

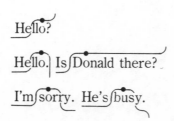

74

Please give him a message.

Excuse me. Wait a minute.

George. Give me a pencil, please.

O.K. What's the message?

The game is tonight.

Adaptation

1. Donald?   *Is Donald there?*
   busy.   *I'm sorry. He's busy.*

   Sandra?   _____ ?
   not here.   _____ . _____ .

   Mr. Taylor?   _____ ?
   sleeping.   _____ . _____ .

   Jane and Bill?   _____ ?
   working.   _____ . _____ .

   Mr. Donaldson?   _____ ?
   busy.   _____ . _____ .

2. Helen. a pencil.   *Helen. Give me a pencil please.*
   message/slowly.   *Please repeat the message slowly.*

   David. a pen.   _____ . _____ .
   number/clearly.   _____ . 75

Alice. a piece of paper. ————— . ————————————— .
name/slowly.   ————————————————————— .

Peter. a card.   ————— . ————————————— .
address/more slowly.   ————————————————————— .

Ann. my notebook.   ————— . ————————————— .
last name/more clearly.   ————————————————————— .

Study 1

Requests: *Please give him a message. Don't forget.*

Notice the form of the requests:

Affirmative:

> **Listen.**
> **Be** quiet.
> **Study** the lesson.
> **Answer** me.

Affirmative requests begin with the simple
form of the verb **(listen, be, study).**

Negative:

> **Don't** talk.
> **Don't** forget the game.
> **Don't** tell me.

Negative requests begin with **don't (do not).**

Practice

Make a negative and then an affirmative request.

listen to the music. *Don't listen to the music.*
to me. *Listen to me.*

read the newspaper. _____ .
your book. _____ .

speak fast. _____ .
slowly. _____ .

repeat the story. _____ .
the message. _____ .

answer the door. _____ .
the phone. _____ .

sit on the floor. _____ .
here. _____ .

give me a pencil. _____ .
a pen. _____ .

Study 2

Polite Requests: *Please repeat the message.*

Notice the position of **please:**

Affirmative:

Please repeat the number.
Please give me a pencil.
Repeat the number, **please.**
Give me a pencil, **please.**

Negative:

> **Please** don't forget.
> **Please** don't tell me.
> Don't forget, **please.**
> Don't tell me, **please.**

Use **please** before or after a request.

Practice

Make a negative and then an affirmative request. Use **please** at the beginning of the first request, and at the end of the second request.

stand on the chair.   *Please don't stand on the chair.*
on the floor,   *Stand on the floor, please.*

sit on the floor.   _____ .
on the chair,   _____ , _____ .

speak fast.   _____ .
more slowly,   _____ , _____ .

leave a message.   _____ .
your number,   _____ , _____ .

repeat the message.   _____ .
the name,   _____ , _____ .

tell me your problem.   _____ .
the story,   _____ , _____ .

Study 3

Object pronouns: *Excuse me.*

Notice the object pronouns **me, him, her, us,** etc.:

I'm busy.	Excuse **me.**
Watch your brother.	Watch **him.**
Ask Jane.	Ask **her.**
Write the lesson.	Write **it.**
Tell Frank and me.	Tell **us.**
Open your books.	Open **them.**

The object form of

I	is	**me**
you		**you**
he		**him**
she		**her**
it		**it**
we		**us**
you		**you**
they		**them**

Practice

Repeat the sentence and make a request using the correct object pronoun.

The door is open.

Close ___*it*___ .

George is in the hospital.

Visit _____ .

The lessons are important.

Study _____ .

Sandra is playing tennis.

Watch _____ .

The sandwich is good.

Eat _____ .

The saleswoman is here.

Ask ___*her*___ .

Helen and I are dancing.

Watch _____ .

The book is interesting.

Read _____ .

I'm singing.

Listen to _____ .

Jack is an interesting person.

Talk to _____ .

79

Study 4

Verbs with two objects: *Give me a pencil.*

Notice the position of the two objects:

Give	a pencil	**to me.**
Give	**me**	a pencil.
Write	a letter	**to him.**
Write	**him**	a letter.
Tell	a story	**to us.**
Tell	**us**	a story.

Use **to** with the object pronoun after a direct object:
Give a pencil to me.
Omit **to** with the object pronoun before a direct object:
Give me a pencil.

Practice

1. Change the model sentence according to the pictures.

Please give me *the book.*

Please _____ .   Please _____ .

Please _____ .   Please _____ .

2. Make polite requests with **to** and the object pronoun. Then say the sentence again without **to**. Use the pictures as cues.

give

Please give the pencil to him.
Please give him the pencil.

read

Please read the book to her.
Please read her the book.

tell

_____ .
_____ .

read

_____ .
_____ .

write

_____ .
_____ .

82

give

John and me (us)

_____ .
_____ .

tell

the time

_____ .
_____ .

write

_____ .
_____ .

Study 5

The colors: *red, yellow, blue, . . .*

Learn the names of the colors:

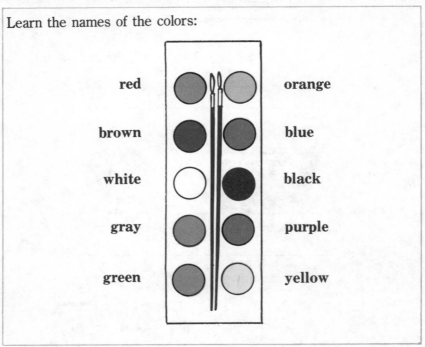

red	orange
brown	blue
white	black
gray	purple
green	yellow

Practice

1. Tell the color of the items below:

apple   bananas

The apple is red.   *The bananas are yellow.*

grapes

pear

orange

strawberries

pepper

carrots

potatoes

tomato

2. Complete the sentences below by adding the appropriate color adjective.

He's wearing a _____ shirt.

They're wearing _____ coats.

She's painting a _____ flower.

He's buying a _____ hat.

They're eating _____ apples.

She's wearing _____ shoes.

He's driving a _____ car.   She's giving him an _____ book.

3. Answer the questions according to the pictures. Use a color adjective before the noun in your answer.

What is he wearing?
He's wearing a green shirt.

What are they eating?
_____ .

What are they wearing?

What is she buying?

_____ .   _____ .

What is he painting?

_____ .

What is he giving her?

_____ .

What is he eating?

_____ .

What is she driving?

_____ .

Study 6

Questions about colors: *What color is the house?*

Notice the formation of the question:

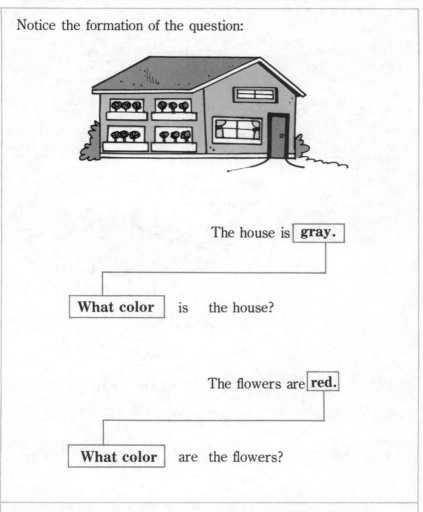

The house is gray.

What color   is   the house?

The flowers are red.

What color   are   the flowers?

To ask questions about colors, use **what + color** at the
beginning of the question.

Practice

This is a picture of Richard's house. What color are the things in the picture? Form a question using the cues, and answer it according to the picture.

sky?
What color is the sky?
It's blue.

clouds?
What color are the clouds?
They're white.

house?
_____ ?
_____ .

door?
_____ ?
_____ .

flowers?
_____ ?
_____ .

grass?   _____ ?

_____ .

chairs?   _____ ?

_____ .

car?   _____ ?

_____ .

Speak

1. **Francis:** Please tell me a story.
   Elizabeth: About your father?
   Francis: No. Tell me a story about you.
   Elizabeth: I have an interesting story.
   Francis: Is it long?
   Elizabeth: No. It's short.
   Francis: Please tell it to me.

2. Richard: What are you doing?
  Donald: I'm making cookies.
Richard: Are you a good cook?
  Donald: No, I'm not. But my cookies are good.

Read

Dear Maria,

   How are you? My family and I are fine. Robert and Susan are now in college. Robert is studying languages. Susan is studying chemistry. It's a difficult subject, but she likes it. I am now captain of the soccer team. We practice every day after school. We have an excellent team.

What are you doing? Please tell me. Write me a long letter. Send me pictures of you and your family. Don't forget. Please give your family my love.

Your friend,
Richard

Answer the questions.

1. What is Richard writing?
2. Where are Robert and Susan?
3. Who is studying chemistry?
4. What is Robert studying?
5. Is Richard captain of the soccer team?
6. How is the soccer team?

Pronounce

Contrast [z] and [s].

zip [z]   Zip the zipper.

sip [s]   Sip the soup.

please
memorize
easy
music
Rose
songs

lesson
class
students
sit
sing
tourists

Please memorize the lesson.
Is the lesson easy?
Yes, it is.

This is a music class.
The students are singing songs.
Rose and Susan are sitting together.

Unit 7

Conversation:
Talking about occupations

Richard

Donald Taylor

Donald: What's Barbara Stern?
Richard: She's a translator. She works at the United Nations.
Donald: My brother works at the United Nations.
Richard: Is he a translator?
Donald: No. He's a guide.
Richard: What's his name?
Donald: His name is Dennis.

What's Barbara Stern?

She's a translator.

She works at the United Nations.

My brother works at the United Nations.

Is he a translator?

No. He's a guide.

What's his name?

His name is Dennis.

Adaptation

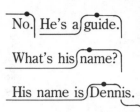

1. Barbara Stern?   *What's Barbara Stern?*
   a translator.   *She's a translator.*
   at the United Nations. *She works at the United Nations.*

Alice Hill?   _____ ?

a nurse.   _____ .

in a hospital. _____ .

Peter Jones?   _____ ?

a worker.   _____ .

in a factory.   _____ .   95

 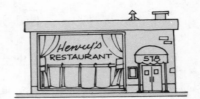

David Graham?   _____?
a waiter.   _____.
in a restaurant.   _____.

2. my brother/at the   *My brother works at the*
United Nations.   *United Nations.*
translator?   *Is he a translator?*
guide.   *No, he's a guide.*

Julia/in a hospital.   _____.
nurse?   _____?
doctor.   _____.

Janet/in a school.   _____.
teacher?   _____?
secretary.   _____.

Helen/in a garage.   _____.
mechanic?   _____?
bookkeeper.   _____.

David/in a restaurant.   _____.
cook?   _____?
96   waiter.   _____?

Study 1

Regular present tense: *She works at the United Nations.*

Notice the verb forms:

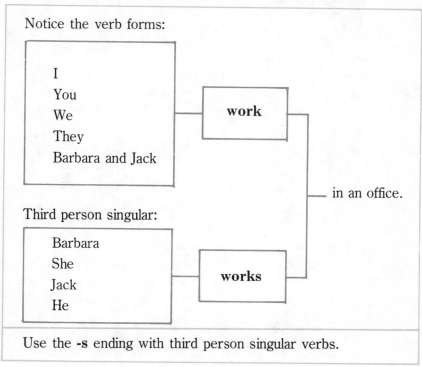

Third person singular:

Use the **-s** ending with third person singular verbs.

Practice

1. What do the people in the pictures do every day?

I'm a teacher.   He's a mechanic.

I ____*teach*____ English.   He ____*works*____ in a garage.

97

We're students.
We _____ geography.

She's a singer.
She _____ in a club.

They're musicians.
They _____ the guitar.

He's a waiter.
He _____ in a restaurant.

I'm a scientist.
I _____ in a laboratory.

Jane is a saleswoman.
She _____ in a store.

2. Make sentences about the people below using the words and pictures as cues.

Janice

every day

Janice plays the piano every day.

Richard   to  every evening

Donald

_____ .

I  every night

_____ .

He  to every week

Carmen

_____ .

You  in the morning

_____ .

We  in the evening

_____ . 99

Margaret  Japanese in

They  the German newspaper in

Study 2

Third person singular of present tense: *He reads.*   *She speaks.*   *It changes.*

Notice the pronunciation of the third person:

I. Pronounce [z] with voiced final sounds [n, d, j, etc.].

The third person of	listen read study understand	is	listens. reads. studies. understands.

II. Pronounce [s] with voiceless final sounds [k, t, etc.].

The third person of	speak write	is	speaks. writes.

III. Pronounce [iz] with the final sounds [s, z, š, ž, č, ǰ].

The third person of

practice	is	practices.
memorize		memorizes.
wash		washes.
relax		relaxes.
change		changes.

Spelling:

In group III above, notice that verbs not ending in **-e**
take an **-es** ending (**wash ▶ washes, relax ▶ relaxes,** etc.).

Learn these irregular verb forms:

The third person of

have	is	has.
go		goes.
do		does.

Practice

Barbara Stern works hard all day at the United Nations. After work
she goes home. Tell about her activities after work.

go home

▶ *She goes home.*

change her ciothes

▶

sit down

▶

relax

▶

read the newspaper

▶

cook dinner

▶

eat dinner

▶

101

do the dishes

▶

telephone a friend

▶

watch the news

▶

go to bed

▶

Study 3

The days of the week: *Sunday, Monday, . . .*

Memorize the days of the week:

Sunday
Monday
Tuesday
Wednesday
Thursday
Friday
Saturday

Practice

Dennis Taylor has an interesting job at the United Nations, but when he's not at work he has very different activities. What are his activities each day?

Monday: swim
▶ *He swims on Monday.*
Tuesday: practice the guitar

▶

Wednesday: study photography

▶

Thursday: go to the movies

▶

Friday: eat in a restaurant

▶

Saturday morning: have a guitar lesson

▶

Saturday afternoon: wash his clothes

▶

Sunday: play tennis

▶

Speak

Barbara speaks about herself in the first person:

"I'm Barbara Stern. I'm a translator. I speak English and Chinese. I work in an office at the United Nations. I translate letters. I read letters in Chinese. I write letters in English. I practice Chinese in the office, and I read Chinese newspapers at home. I speak English to Dennis."

Dennis speaks about Barbara in the third person:

"She's Barbara Stern. She's a translator. She speaks English and Chinese. She works in an office at the United Nations. She translates letters. She reads letters in Chinese. She writes letters in English. She practices Chinese in the office, and she reads Chinese newspapers at home. She speaks English to me."

Dennis speaks about himself in the first person:

"I'm Dennis Taylor. I work at the United Nations. I'm a guide. I guide visitors. I speak English and Spanish. I read Spanish novels. I understand them. I write letters in English."

A student tells about Dennis Taylor:

"He's Dennis Taylor. He works at the United Nations. . . ."

Other students continue in the same way. One student speaks about himself or herself in the first person, and another student reports it in the third person.

Read

Robert, Sylvia, and Vincent are friends. They are learning Spanish in the evening. They listen to the teacher, and they speak Spanish in class. At home they read Spanish books.

Robert works in a garage. He fixes cars. He's a mechanic. Vincent is a singer. He sings in a club. He sings English songs, Italian songs, and Spanish songs. Sylvia is a teacher. She works in a high school. She teaches chemistry.

Answer the questions.

1. What are Robert, Sylvia, and Vincent learning?
2. What do they read at home?

3. Are Robert and Sylvia singers?
4. What is Robert?
5. What does he fix?
6. Where does Vincent sing?
7. Does Sylvia work in a club?
8. What does she teach?

Pronounce

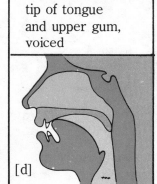

exploded between
tip of tongue
and upper gum,
voiced

day [d]

[d]

day
Donal**d**
Davi**d**
doctor
doing
difficult
me**d**icine
Lon**d**on
stu**d**y

Is Donald a doctor?
Yes, he's a doctor of medicine.
He's Donald Day, M.D.
He's Dr. Donald Day.

Where is David Day?
David is in London.
What is David doing in London?
He's studying difficult subjects.

Unit 8

Conversation:
Ordering dinner at a restaurant

Waiter: Do you want fish or meat?
Bernard: We want fish.
Waiter: Do you want coffee?
Bernard: No, thank you. I want soda.
Waiter: Does the little boy want soda?
Bernard: No, he doesn't. He drinks milk.

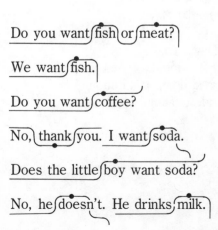

106

Adaptation

1. fish or meat?

Do you want fish or meat?
We want fish.

coffee or tea?

_____?
_____.

milk or cream?

_____?
_____.

rice or potatoes?

_____?
_____.

2. milk?
   coffee.

Do you want milk?
No, thank you. I want coffee.

sugar?
cream.

_____?
___._____.

fish?
meat.

_____?
___._____.

potatoes?

bread.

_____ ?

_____ . _____ .

3. drink milk?

tea.

Does Mary drink milk?

No, she doesn't. She drinks tea.

like soup?

eggs.

_____ ?

_____ . _____ .

eat meat?

fish.

_____ ?

_____ . _____ .

want rice?

potatoes.

_____ ?

_____ . _____ .

Study 1

Negative statements in the present tense: *She doesn't drink milk.*

Notice the negative statements:

Affirmative:

I **drink** coffee.

He **drinks** tea.

108

Negative:

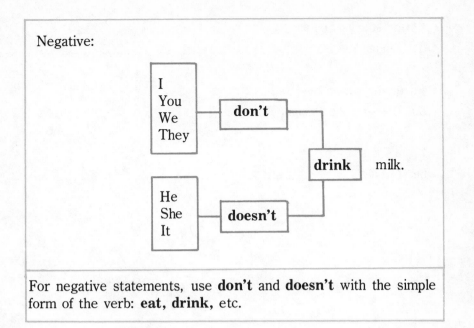

For negative statements, use **don't** and **doesn't** with the simple form of the verb: **eat, drink,** etc.

Practice

Complete the sentence using the negative.

Bernard likes milk,
but Jane doesn't like milk.

The waiter works in the restaurant,
but Bernard and Jane don't work in the restaurant.

You drink coffee,
but I _____ .

I like wine,
but Helen _____ .

Cats eat fish,
but dogs _____ . 109

Carlos speaks Spanish,
but Linda _____ .

Alice works in a hospital,
but Barbara and Dennis _____ .

Dennis has a job,
but Donald _____ .

Study 2

Yes/no questions in the present tense: *Do you want milk?*

Notice the use of **do** and **does** and the form of the verb:

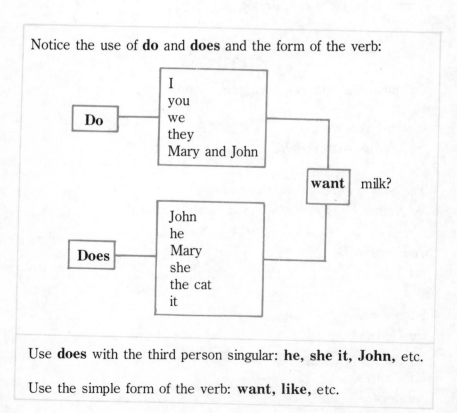

Use **does** with the third person singular: **he, she it, John,** etc.

Use the simple form of the verb: **want, like,** etc.

Practice

1. Ask questions about the following pictures. Use the verb **like** in
   your questions.

Paul

Does Paul like milk?

Richard and Alan

Do Richard and Alan like meat?

Peter

they

_____ ?   _____ ?

you

Lynn

_____ ?   _____ ?

Eve   ice cream   you and Francis   cake

_____ ?   _____ ? 111

2. Ask a question using the cue words and answer it according to the picture. Use the verb **want**.

you/tea or coffee?

Do you want tea or coffee?
I want tea.

he/water or milk?

Does he want water or milk?
He wants water.

she/coffee or tea?

_____?
_____.

they/beer or wine?

_____?
_____.

you/fish or chicken?

_____?
_____.

Virginia/rice or potatoes?

_____?
_____.

John and Helen/fish or meat?  _____ ?

_____ .

you and Helen/soup or eggs? _____ ?

_____ .

you and Philip/water or milk? _____ ?

_____ .

the cat/fish or meat? _____ ?

_____ .

you/hot milk or cold milk? _____ ?

_____ .

Study 3

Short answers in the present tense: *Yes, I do. No, he doesn't.*

Notice the affirmative and negative short answers:

Affirmative:

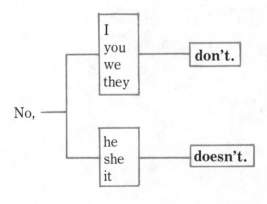

Do or **does** completes the affirmative short answer.

Negative:

No,

| I you we they | don't. |
| he she it | doesn't. |

Don't or **doesn't** completes the negative short answer.
Don't and **doesn't** are the contractions of **do not** and **does not**.

Practice

Answer the questions with affirmative or negative short answers, according to the pictures.

Do Barbara and Dennis work
at the United Nations?
▶ *Yes, they do.*
Does Dennis work in an office?
▶ *No, he doesn't.*

Dennis   Barbara

Does Robert work in a garage?
▶
Do Sylvia and Vincent work
in a garage?
▶

Robert   Sylvia   Vincent

Does Philip study mathematics?
▶
Does he like mathematics?
▶

Philip

Does Jack like astronomy?
▶
Does he read astronomy books?
▶

Jack

Do cats eat fish?

▶

Do they drink coffee?

▶

Do you like the painting?

▶

Do I paint well?

▶

Speak

1. **Philip:** Hello, Charles.
    Charles: Hello, Philip.
    Philip: What are you doing?
    Charles: I'm watching the baseball game.
    Philip: Do you like baseball?
    Charles: No, I don't, but my brother does.

2. **Alice:** Where are you going?
    Karen: I'm going to a restaurant.
    Alice: Do you want pizza?
    Karen: Yes, I do.
    Alice: Go to the Pizza House.
    It's an excellent restaurant.

3. **Bernard:** Do you want tea or coffee?
    Jane: I want tea.
    Bernard: Does Mary like coffee?
    Jane: No, she doesn't. She likes milk.

Read

Dinner in New York

Hector and Isabel Rivera are in a restaurant in New York. They are having dinner. They are from Venezuela. They are tourists in the United States. They speak Spanish, but they speak English well too. They are talking to the waiter in English. Isabel is ordering soup, fish, and rice. She likes fish. Hector does not like fish. He wants meat. He is ordering soup, meat, and potatoes. He also wants coffee with dinner. Isabel drinks coffee after dinner, but she wants water right now. They do not want wine or beer. Hector and Isabel like American food. They like the restaurant. The waiter is polite and friendly. They like him too.

Answer the questions.

1. Where are Hector and Isabel?
2. What are they doing?
3. Where are they from?
4. Do they speak English well?
5. What is Isabel ordering?
6. Does Hector like fish?

7. Does he want coffee with dinner?
8. Does Isabel want coffee right now?
9. Do they want wine?
10. Do they like the waiter?

Pronounce

they [ð]	friction between tongue and upper teeth, voiced
	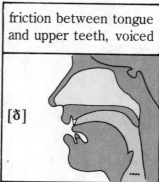

[ð]

this
father
they
mother
the
brother

Is this the father?
Yes. This is the father.

Is this the mother?
Yes. This is the mother.

Are they the brothers?
Yes. They are the brothers.

Unit 9

Conversation: Sightseeing

Helen and Glen Newman

Glen: What is this?
Helen: This is the Museum of Art.
Glen: What's that over there?
Helen: That's the sports stadium.
Glen: And what are those?
Helen: Those are souvenir shops.

What is this?

This is the Museum of Art.

What's that over there?

That's the sports stadium.

And what are those?

Those are souvenir shops.

Adaptation

1. this?   *What is this?*
   Museum of Art.   *This is the Museum of Art.*

   that?   _____?
   post office.   _____.

   this?   _____?
   bus station.   _____.

   that?   _____?
   National Bank.   _____.

   this?   _____?
   information center. _____.

2. that over there?   *What's that over there?*
   the sports stadium.   *That's the sports stadium.*

   those?   *What are those?*
   souvenir shops.   _____.

   that over there?   _____?
   a mailbox.   _____.

   those?   _____?
   taxis.   _____.

   that over there?   _____?
   the subway station. _____.

Study 1

Demonstrative pronouns: *This is the Museum of Art. Those are souvenir shops.*

Notice the use of **this, that, these,** and **those:**

Singular: **This** is an apple.   **That** is a banana.

Plural: **These** are apples.   **Those** are bananas.

This and **these** are used for objects near the speaker.

That and **those** are used for objects away from the speaker.

Practice

1. The objects are away from you. Answer with **that** or **those.**

What is this?

That's a pencil.

What are these?

Those are apples.

What is this?

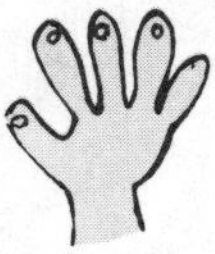

_____ .

What are these?

_____ .

What is this?

_____ .

What are these?

_____ .

2. The objects are near you. Answer with **this** or **these**.

What is that?   *This is a letter.*

What are those?   *These are bananas.*

What is that?   _____.

What are those?   _____.

What is that?   _____.

What are those?   _____.

Study 2

Parts of the body: *arms, legs, . . .*

He has

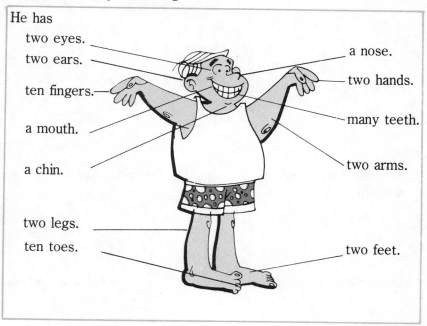

two eyes.
two ears.
ten fingers.
a mouth.
a chin.
two legs.
ten toes.

a nose.
two hands.
many teeth.
two arms.
two feet.

Practice

1. Ask and answer questions about the pictures according to their position.

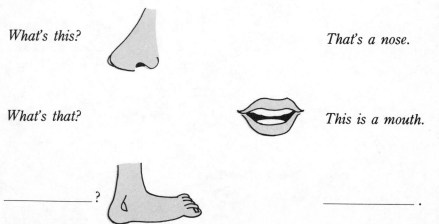

What's this?   *That's a nose.*

What's that?   *This is a mouth.*

_____ ?   _____ .

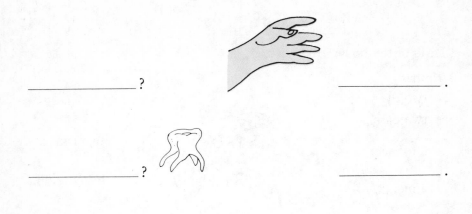

_____ ? _____ .

_____ ? _____ .

2. Ask and answer questions about the pictures according to their position:

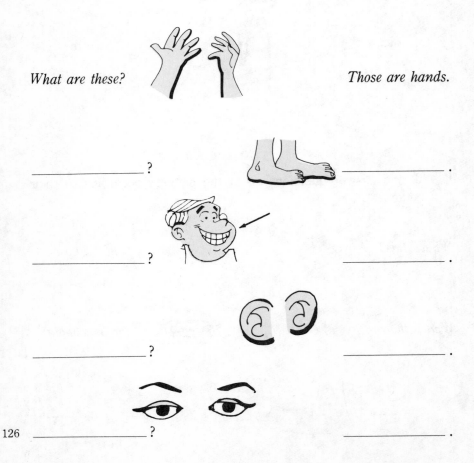

What are these?   *Those are hands.*

_____ ? _____ .

_____ ? _____ .

_____ ? _____ .

_____ ? _____ .

Study 3

Irregular plurals: *These are children.*

Learn these irregular plurals:

The plural of

	is	
man		**men.**
woman		**women.**
child		**children.**
foot		**feet.**
tooth		**teeth.**
person		**people.**

Practice

Give a sentence in the singular. Then make the sentence plural.

This is a tooth.   *These are teeth.*

This is a person.   _____.

_____.   _____.

_____.   _____.

_____.   _____.

_____ . _____ .

_____ . _____ .

_____ . _____ .

Study 4

Numbers 1 to 20: *one, two, three, . . .*

Learn these numbers:

1 one	11 eleven
2 two	12 twelve
3 three	13 thirteen
4 four	14 fourteen
5 five	15 fifteen
6 six	16 sixteen
7 seven	17 seventeen
8 eight	18 eighteen
9 nine	19 nineteen
10 ten	20 twenty

Stress the last syllable of numbers ending in **-teen: thirteen, four-teen,** etc.

Practice

1. Count from one to twenty.

2. Read these numbers aloud.
   5, 10, 15, 20   3, 6, 9, 12
   2, 4, 8, 16   1, 7, 11, 13

Study 5

There is/there are: *There are plates on the table.*

Notice the use of **there is** and **there are** to tell about the picture below:

There is	a	cat	on the table.
There's	a	cake	on the table.
There are	two	glasses	on the table.
There are		plates	on the table.

There is is followed by a singular noun.

There are is followed by a plural noun.

After the noun, there is usually a phrase like **on the table,** which answers the question **where?**

There's is the contraction of **there is.**

Practice

Complete the sentences below to tell what is in each picture.

There's a picture on the wall.

There are two eggs on the plate.

_____ on the table.

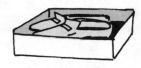

_____ in the box.

_____ in the basket.

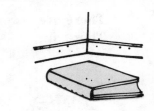

_____ on the floor.

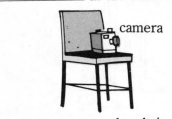
camera

_____ on the chair.

_____ on the table.

130 _____ in the family.

_____ in the bag.

Study 6

Questions with **there is/there are:** *Is there a picture on the wall?*

Notice the formation of the questions:

There **is** a cat on the table.

Is there a cat on the table?

There **are** plates on the table.

Are there plates on the table?

Put **is** and **are** in the first position in the question.

Practice

Glen and Helen Newman are visiting Washington, D.C. this week. They don't know Washington very well, so they are asking many questions about it. What are they asking? Use the words as cues.

Helen

Glen

subway   *Is there a subway in Washington?*

buses   *Are there buses in Washington?*

art museum   _____ ?

theaters   _____ ?

sports stadium   _____ ? 131

souvenir shops	_____ ?
park	_____ ?
nice hotels	_____ ?
good restaurants	_____ ?
nice people	_____ ?

Study 7

Short answers with **there is/there are:** *Yes, there is. No, there isn't.*

Notice the short answers to the questions below:

Is there an art museum in Washington?	**Yes, there is.**
Is there an art museum in Greenville?	**No, there isn't.**
Are there theaters in Washington?	**Yes, there are.**
Are there theaters in Greenville?	**No, there aren't.**

Isn't is the contraction of **is not.**

Aren't is the contraction of **are not.**

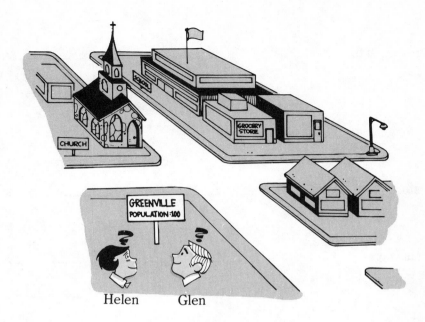

Helen   Glen

Practice

Glen and Helen Newman have a friend from Greenville, Ohio. They are asking the friend about Greenville. What are they asking? What is the friend answering? Use the words as cues, and answer the questions according to the picture.

hospital

Is there a hospital in Greenville?
No, there isn't.

houses

Are there houses in Greenville?
Yes, there are.

school

_____ ?

_____ .

college

_____ ?

_____ . 133

restaurants _____ ?

_____ .

post office _____ ?

_____ .

store _____ ?

_____ .

subway _____ ?

_____ .

buses _____ ?

_____ .

taxis _____ ?

_____ .

church _____ ?

_____ .

people _____ ?

_____ .

factories _____ ?

_____ .

Study 8

The contractions **isn't** and **aren't**: *We aren't working.*

Notice the possible contractions of **be + not:**

I am not busy now.	▶ I'm not busy now.
We are not working.	▶ We're not working. We **aren't** working.
She is not here.	▶ She's not here. She **isn't** here.
Are you hungry?	▶ No, I'm not.
Are they eating?	▶ No, they're not. No, they **aren't**.
Is he unhappy?	▶ No, he's not. No, he **isn't**.

Are not is often contracted to **aren't**.

Is not is often contracted to **isn't**.

I am not has only one contraction: **I'm not**.

Aren't and **isn't** are often used in short answers.

Practice

Answer these questions with negative short answers using **isn't** and **aren't** when possible.

Is Helen Newman in Chicago now?
▶ *No, she isn't.*
Are Helen and Glen at home this week?
▶ *No, they aren't.*
Is Jack Newman in Washington?

Are Helen and Glen visiting Greenville now?

▶

Is Greenville a big city?

▶

Are there restaurants in Greenville?

▶

Is there an art museum in Greenville?

▶

Is Washington a small town?

▶

Are you visiting Washington this week?

▶

Are Washington and Greenville in Canada?

▶

Are you tourists?

▶

Am I going to Chicago this week?

▶

Speak

1.   **Jack:** Look at these pictures.

    Charles: Is that your brother?

    Jack: No, it isn't. It's my cousin.

    Charles: What's that?

    Jack: This is a shark.

    Charles: Those are big teeth!

2. Saleswoman: Do you want this camera, ma'am?

        Helen: Yes. I want this camera and that film.

                  Are there photography books in this store?

Saleswoman: No, there aren't. But there is a bookstore near here.

Read

    We are in Washington. We are visiting the National Museum of Art. This is the museum guide. His name is Mr. Thompson. Mr. Thompson is showing us very beautiful things. There are many old paintings in the museum. There is an interesting sculpture in this room. We are asking Mr. Thompson many questions. "What's this? What's that? What are those?" Mr. Thompson listens to the questions, and then he answers,   137

"That's a modern sculpture. It doesn't have a title. This is an old painting by a famous artist. These are small Greek statues."

Mr. Thompson asks us, "Do you like ancient coins?" Glen says, "I do. Are these ancient coins?" Mr. Thompson answers, "Yes. Those are ancient Chinese coins."

Answer the questions.

1. Who is the museum guide?
2. What is he showing them?
3. Does the sculpture have a title?
4. What are the statues?
5. Who likes ancient coins?

Pronounce

Contrast [d] and [ð].

day [d]	they [ð]

Davi**d**	**th**is
Donal**d**	**th**at
Edward	**th**eir
Doris	fa**th**er
goo**d**	mo**th**er
ba**d**	bro**th**er

138

David and Donald are brothers.
This is their family.

Their father is Edward.
Their mother is Doris.

Is this Donald?
Then, this is David,
and this is their father.

Is this their mother?
Then, this is their sister, Diane.

Unit 10

Conversation:
Planning a program

Lynn   Jim   John   Mary   David   Carlos

Philip: Who announces Mary's song?
  Ann: John announces it.
Philip: What happens after her song?
  Ann: Carlos reads his poem.
Philip: Who comes after him?
  Ann: Lynn and David. They play their guitars.
Philip: O.K. That's fine.

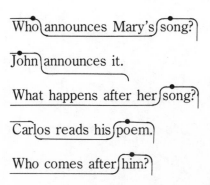

Lynn and David. They play their guitars.

O.K. That's fine.

Adaptation

1. announces Mary's song?
   John

   Who announces Mary's song?
   John announces it.

   listens to Mary's song?
   Philip

   _____?
   _____.

   announces Carlos's poem?
   Richard

   _____?
   _____.

   likes Carlos's poem?
   Lynn and David

   _____?
   _____.

2. after her song?
   Carlos reads, poem.

   What happens after her song?
   Carlos reads his poem.

   after his poem?
   Ann tells/joke.

   _____?
   _____.

   after her joke?
   Ann and Philip do/dance.

   _____?
   _____.

   after their dance?
   Lynn and David play/
   guitars.

   _____?
   _____.

3. him?
   Lynn and David.
   play/guitars.

   Who comes after him?
   Lynn and David.
   They play their guitars.

   you?
   Ann and Tom.
   sing/song.

   _____?
   _____.
   _____. 141

them?   _____?
Roger and Rachel.   _____.
tell/jokes.   _____.

her?   _____?
Carlos and Carmen.   _____.
read/poem.   _____.

us?   _____?
He and Sylvia.   _____.
do/dance.   _____.

Study 1

Possessive adjectives: *This is his brother.*

Notice the possessive forms:

This is
my
your
his
her
its
our
your
their
brother. These are
my
your
his
her
its
our
your
their
brothers.

Possessive forms change for each person:

I	**my**	we	**our**
you	**your**	you	**your**
he	**his**	they	**their**
she	**her**		
it	**its**		

They do not change for plural nouns:
This is **my** brother.
These are **my** brothers.

142

Practice

1. Complete the sentences. Use the pictures as cues.

This is _____*my*_____ guitar.

I like _____*his*_____ shoes.

I know _____ sister.

I want _____ car.

The cat wants _____ milk.

143

We like _____ houses.

You have _____ pencils.

You have _____ hat.

He loves _____ dress.

2. Make sentences with the same meaning, using the possessive.

He has big eyes. *His eyes are big.*

She has a beautiful mouth. _____.

I have a new car. _____.

It has a long tail. _____ .

You have good teeth. _____ .

They have big hands. _____ .

We have a new house. _____ .

You have long arms. _____ .

Study 2

Possessive forms of nouns: *John announces Mary's song.*

Notice the singular possessive:

This is
the girl's	friend.
John's	friend.
Francis's	friend.
the child's	friend.

These are
the girl's	friends.
John's	friends.
Francis's	friends.
the child's	friends.

Add **'s** to form the possessive of **all** singular nouns.

Notice the plural possessive:

This is
| the girls' | friend. |
| the doctors' | friend. |

These are
| the girls' | friends. |
| the doctors' | friends. |

145

This is	the children's the women's	friend. friend.

These are	the children's the women's	friends. friends.

Add **'** to form the possessive of plural nouns that end in **s.**
Add **'s** to form the possessive of plural nouns that do **not** end in **s.**

Practice

1. Identify the objects and the owners in the pictures. Use sentences like the examples below.

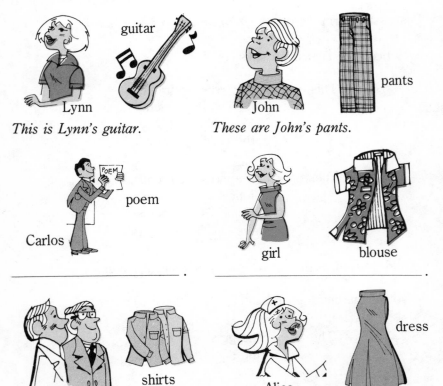

guitar

Lynn

This is Lynn's guitar.

pants

John

These are John's pants.

poem

Carlos

girl

blouse

_____ .

men

shirts

Alice

dress

_____ .

146 _____ . _____ .

Glen

student

Dennis

Sandra

boys

doctor

2. Identify the objects and the owners. Then describe the objects. Use the appropriate possessive adjective in the second sentence.

Helen

These are Glen's teeth.
His teeth are white.

This is Helen's camera.
Her camera is new.

Mary

me

_____.

big.

beautiful.

you

Mr. Thompson

_____.

black.

young

children

us

_____.

interesting.

old.

Study 3

Pronunciation of possessives: *John's, Robert's, Alice's*

Pronounce [z] after a voiced final sound:

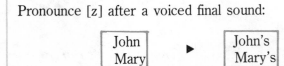

| John | ▶ | John's |
| Mary | | Mary's |

Pronounce [s] after a voiceless final sound:

Robert Philip	►	Robert's Philip's	

Pronounce [iz] after [s, z, š, ž, č, ǰ]:

Alice the coach the judge	►	Alice's the coach's the judge's	

Possessives of both singular and plural nouns are pronounced like the plurals of nouns:

Pronounce	the mechanic's the waitress's the coaches' the workers'	like	the mechanics. the waitresses. the coaches. the workers.

Practice

Pronounce the possessive.

John has a book.
► *It's John's book.*

Philip has a dictionary.
► *It's Philip's dictionary.*

Alice is writing a letter.
►

Francis has a pen.
►

Janet has a cat.
►

Jack has a car.
►

Sandra is drinking tea.
▶

Lynn is playing the guitar.
▶

The judge has a problem.
▶

Study 4

Subject questions: *Who announces Mary's song?*

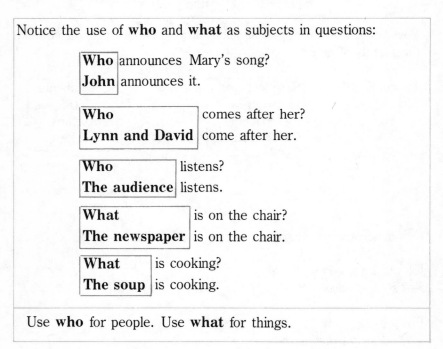

Notice the use of **who** and **what** as subjects in questions:

Who announces Mary's song?
John announces it.

Who comes after her?
Lynn and David come after her.

Who listens?
The audience listens.

What is on the chair?
The newspaper is on the chair.

What is cooking?
The soup is cooking.

Use **who** for people. Use **what** for things.

Practice

Ask a subject question on each sentence. Then answer it according to the picture.

Linda

London

Bill doesn't live in London.
▶ *Who lives in London?*
▶ *Linda lives in London.*

The cream isn't on the table.
▶ *What is on the table?*
▶ *The milk is on the table.*

Alice

Helen doesn't want milk.
▶
▶

The dog isn't on the table.
▶
▶

Jack

Helen and Glen don't need money.
▶
▶

The dress isn't expensive.
▶
▶

Bill isn't playing basketball.
▶
▶

Lynn

The soup isn't hot.
▶
▶

John doesn't work in Chicago.
▶
▶

David

Speak

1. **Lynn:** Is this your skirt?
   Alice: No, it's not. My skirt is long.
   Lynn: Is it Mary's skirt?
   Alice: Yes, it is. Her skirt is short.

2. **Lynn:** Who is watching television?
Charles: Richard is.
   Lynn: What is he watching?
Charles: The football game.

3. **Nicole:** Who has an English dictionary?
   Charles: I have an English-French dictionary.
   Nicole: No. I need an English dictionary.
   Charles: Use Mary's dictionary.

Read

Harry, Karen, and Ralph are at Phil and Mary Cappa's party. Phil is their boss, and the party is at his house. Phil and Mary like big parties, and there are twenty-five people at their house. Mary is playing the piano. Phil is telling a joke and laughing. Their daughter is playing the guitar, and their son is singing. Harry and Karen are dancing. Ralph is drinking punch and eating peanuts. This is an excellent party.

Answer the questions:

1. Who is at Phil and Mary Cappa's party?
2. Who likes big parties?
3. Who is playing the piano?
4. What is Phil doing?
5. What are their children doing?
6. Who is dancing?
7. Who is eating?

Pronounce

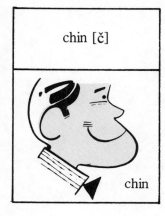

chin [č]

chin

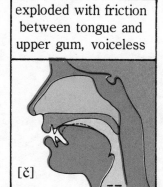

exploded with friction between tongue and upper gum, voiceless

[č]

chin
tea**ch**er
Charles
Fren**ch**
Chile
bea**ch**

Charles is a teacher.
He teaches French.
He teaches in Chile.

Chile has beautiful beaches.
There are children at the beach.
A child hurts his chin.
Charles is the child's teacher.

Key to Pronunciation Symbols

Vowels and Diphthongs

[iy]	sheep
[i]	ship
[ey]	pain
[e]	net
[æ]	pan, man
[a]	father, socks
[ow]	phone
[ɔ]	Paul, all
[uw]	pool, two
[u]	foot, pull
[ə́]	nut
[ə]	across
[ay]	buy, eye
[aw]	mouth
[ɔy]	boy

Consonants

Voiceless:

[pʰ]	pan	[p]	nap
[tʰ]	tan	[t]	bat
[kʰ]	can	[k]	back
[f]	fan		
[θ]	three, ether		
[s]	sip		
[š]	shin		
[č]	chin		

Voiced:

[b]	band
[d]	day
[g]	good
[v]	van
[ð]	they, either
[z]	zip
[ž]	leisure
[ǰ]	jam
[l]	light
[r]	right
[m]	some
[n]	sun
[ŋ]	sung

157

Semiconsonants

[y] **y**am, **y**es
[w] **w**ood
[h] **h**ood, **h**e

Syllabic Consonants

[l̩] app**le**
[m̩] stop **'em** (stop them)
[n̩] did**n't**

Stress and Intonation

Syllable stress (within a word): [']

Phrase or sentence stress: [-•-]

Intonation levels:

    4 extra high ——————
    3 high   ——————
    2 mid   ——————
    1 low   ——————

Endings for intonation levels:
    rise   —————⌐
    sustain   ——————
    fade out   ——————⌐

Examples of stress and intonation:

yes/no question: ₂ Is he ∫home?³

information question: ₂ Where³ is he?₁

statement: ₂ He's ∫sleep³ing.₁

with emphasis: ₂ He's ∫still⁴ sleeping!₁

158

Vocabulary List

These are the words introduced in Book 1. The number after each word indicates the page on which it first appears. If a word can be used as more than one part of speech, the way it is used in the text is indicated as follows: n = noun, v = verb, adj = adjective, adv = adverb, prep = preposition, pron = pronoun, and conj = conjunction.

a, 1
about, 24
above, 101
absent, 7
activity, 60
add, 69
address, 76
adjective, 69
adverb, 69
affirmative, 4
after, 31
afternoon, 103
agent, 25
Aki, 3
Alan, 111
Albert, 2
Alice, 8
all, 101
always, 72
am, 15
American, 1
an, 49
ancient, 138
and, 4
Ann, 10
announce, 140
answer (v), 6
apple, 49
are, 13
Argentina, 9
arm, 125

art, 52
artist, 138
as, 81
ask, 6
astronomy, 69
Asunción, 9
at, 34
audience, 150
away, 122

bad, 138
bag (n), 130
banana, 49
bank (n), 121
Barbara, 27
baseball, 116
basement, 72
basket, 130
basketball, 152
be, 15
beach, 155
beautiful, 15
bed, 38
bedroom, 59
beer, 112
before, 78
begin, 29
below, 16
Berlin, 19
Bernard, 106
between, 105

big, 35
Bill, 2
black, 85
blouse, 146
blue, 84
body, 125
Bogotá, 9
Bolivia, 9
Bonn, 46
book, 46
bookkeeper, 96
bookstore, 137
boss (n), 154
Boston, 11
both, 149
box (n), 130
boy, 46
Brasilia, 9
Brazil, 9
Brazilian, 3
bread, 108
British Honduras, 9
brother, 13
brown, 84
Buenos Aires, 9
bus (n), 46
bus station, 121
busy, 56
but, 25
buy, 86
by, 69

cake, 111
California, 45
camera, 130
Canada, 9
capital, 54
(Mary) Cappa, 154
captain, 92
car, 69

Caracas, 9
card, 76
cards, 72
Carlos, 10
Carmen, 2
Carol, 72
Carolyn, 2
carrot, 50
cat, 49
center (n), 121
chair, 78
change (v), 100
Charles, 24
chemistry, 53
Chicago, 9
chicken, 112
child, 127
children, 127
Chile, 9
chin, 125
China, 43
Chinese, 103
Christine, 8
church, 133
city, 19
class, 6
classification, 44
classified, 46
clean (v), 72
clear (adj), 69
clearly, 69
clock (n), 50
close (v), 79
clothes, 101
cloud (n), 90
club (n), 70
coach (n), 149
coat (n), 86
coffee, 64
coin, 138
cold (adj), 113

college, 92
(Mr.) Collins, 44
Colombia, 5
Colombian, 5
color (n), 85
come, 101
complete (v), 86
computer, 56
computer programmer, 56
consonant, 49
construct (v), 2
continue, 19
contraction, 4
contrast (n), 6
contrast (v), 36
conversation, 4
cook (n), 21
cook (v), 101
cookie, 92
correct, 18
Costa Rica, 9
count (v), 129
country, 35
cousin, 14
cream, 107
cry (v), 62
Cuba, 9
cue, 2

dance (n), 141
dance (v), 64
daughter, 154
David, 34
day, 92
(Donald) Day, 105
dear (adj), 92
delicious, 51
Dennis, 72
describe, 64
Diane, 139
dictionary, 149

different, 102
difficult, 22
dinner, 53
dish, 72
do, 57
doesn't, 108
doctor, 3
dog, 20
Dominican Republic, 9
Donald, 10
(Mr.) Donaldson, 75
don't, 76
door, 77
Doris, 138
down (sit down), 101
Dr. (doctor), 54
dress (n), 52
drink (v), 63
drive (v), 87
Dublin, 19

each, 23
ear, 50
East Germany, 19
easy, 22
eat, 59
Ecuador, 9
Edith, 26
Edward, 24
egg, 59
eight, 72
eighteen, 128
eleven, 128
Elizabeth, 24
end (v), 29
ending (n), 97
engineer, 56
England, 4
English, 1
etc. (etcetera), 78
Eugene, 26

161

Europe, 35
Eve, 26
evening, 99
every, 92
exam, 10
example, 146
excellent, 53
excuse (v), 74
Excuse me, 74
expensive, 151
eye, 49

factory, 53
family, 25
famous, 138
fast (adv), 60
father (n), 13
feet, 125
fifteen, 128
film (n), 137
final, 100
fine (adj), 7
finger, 125
first (adj), 6
fish (n), 106
five, 128
fix (v), 104
floor, 77
flower (n), 86
following (adj), 6
food, 118
foot, 127
football, 153
for, 32
forget, 76
form (n), 16
form (v), 52
four, 128
fourteen, 128
France, 5

Francis, 7
Frank, 33
French, 3
French Guiana, 9
Friday, 102
friend, 13
friendly, 29
from, 16

game, 54
garage, 96
geography, 53
George, 57
German, 100
Germany, 35
girl, 145
give, 44
glass, 129
Glen, 120
go, 60
good, 35
good morning, 35
(Dr.) Graham, 54
grape, 85
grass, 91
gray, 84
Greece, 36
Greek, 36
green, 84
Greenville, 132
group (n), 101
Guatemala, 9
Guayaquil, 9
guessing game, 54
guide (n), 94
guide (v), 103
guitar, 61
gum, 105
Guyana, 9

Haiti, 9
hand (n), 50
handsome, 15
happen, 140
happy, 7
hard (adv), 69
Harry, 154
has, 101
hat, 86
Havana, 9
have, 72
have a good time, 72
he, 1
Hector, 118
Helen, 57
hello, 35
Henry, 55
her (poss), 140
her (pron), 78
here, 22
herself, 103
hi, 55
high, 17
high school, 104
(Alice) Hill, 11
him, 74
himself, 103
his, 140
history, 53
home, 38
Honduras, 9
horse, 44
hospital, 11
hot, 113
hotel, 132
house (n), 89
how, 38
hungry, 29
hurt (v), 155

I, 15
ice (n), 111
ice cream, 111
identification, 43
identified, 46
identify, 146
I'm, 17
important, 79
in, 4
India, 45
indicate, 46
information, 4
information center, 121
intelligent, 51
interesting, 35
Ireland, 19
irregular, 101
is, 1
Isabel, 118
it, 15
Italian, 5
Italy, 5
its, 142
it's, 17

Jack, 27
(Carolyn) Jackson, 10
Jamaica, 9
Jane, 7
Janet, 96
Janice, 72
Japan, 5
Japanese, 3
Jim, 140
job, 53
John, 7
joke (n), 141
(Peter) Jones, 95
Joseph, 35

judge (n), 149
Julia, 2

Karen, 154
Kathleen, 26
kitchen, 59
know, 71

laboratory, 98
language, 92
La Paz, 9
last (adj), 76
last name, 76
late, 10
laugh (v), 62
lawyer, 21
learn, 101
leave (v), 78
leg, 125
lesson, 53
letter (n), 62
library, 59
like (prep), 2
like (v), 71
Lima, 9
Linda, 1
Lisbon, 19
listen, 62
literature, 53
live (v), 151
living room, 57
location, 44
London, 16
long, 91
look at, 136
Los Angeles, 70
Louise, 7
love (n), 93
love (v), 144
Lynn, 7

ma'am, 137
Madrid, 19
mail (n), 121
mailbox, 121
make (v), 69
man, 20
Manuel, 5
many, 125
map (n), 9
Margaret, 34
Maria, 92
Martha, 55
Mary, 7
math, 10
mathematics, 115
M.D. (medical doctor), 105
me, 74
meaning, 144
meat, 106
mechanic, 5
medicine, 105
memorize, 56
men, 127
message, 74
Mexico, 9
Mexico City, 9
Miami, 9
Michael, 36
milk (n), 70
minute (n), 74
Miss, 45
model (adj), 80
model (n), 2
modern, 138
modifier, 52
Monday, 102
money, 151
Monique, 5
Montevideo, 9
moon, 46
more, 76

morning, 35
most, 69
motel, 72
mother (n), 13
mouth (n), 125
movie, 102
Mr., 44
Mrs., 38
museum, 11
Museum of Art, 120
music, 77
musician, 98
my, 13

name (n), 2
national, 121
National Bank, 121
National Museum of Art, 137
near (prep), 122
necessary, 32
need (v), 71
negative (adj), 31
new, 2
(Jack) Newman, 27
news, 102
newspaper, 62
New York City, 9
Nicaragua, 9
nice, 29
Nick, 36
Nicole, 153
night, 52
nine, 128
nineteen, 128
no, 6
nose, 125
not, 27
notebook, 76
notice (v), 4
noun, 4

novel (n), 103
now, 25
number (n), 75
nurse, 3

object (n), 122
o'clock, 72
of, 4
office, 49
oh, 55
Ohio, 133
O.K., 74
old, 7
omit, 80
on, 46
one, 46
only, 51
open, 79
or, 4
orange (adj), 84
orange (n), 85
order (n), 65
order (v), 106
Oscar, 2
other, 19
Ottawa, 9
our, 142
over, 120
over there, 120
owner, 146

paint (v), 86
painting (n), 116
pair, 6
Panama, 9
pants, 146
paper (n), 76
Paraguay, 9
parent, 24
Paris, 19
park (n), 132

part (n), 125
party (n), 34
Paul, 11
peanut, 154
pear, 50
pen, 75
pencil, 50
people, 65
pepper (n), 85
person, 79
Peru, 9
Peruvian, 3
Peter, 26
Phil, 154
Philip, 1
philosophy, 53
phone (n), 77
photography, 102
phrase, 4
piano, 63
picture (n), 7
piece (of), 76
piece (of music), 72
pilot (n), 36
pizza, 117
Pizza House, 117
place (v), 22
placement, 63
plate, 129
play (v), 61
please (adv), 56
plural, 16
poem, 140
polite, 77
Port-au-Prince, 19
Portugal, 19
position, 6
possessive, 142
post office, 121
potato, 85
practice (v), 72

present (adj), 7
present progressive, 60
present tense, 97
problem, 52
(computer) programmer, 57
(in) progress, 60
pronoun, 18
pronounce, 100
pronunciation, 100
proper, 16
Puerto Rican, 5
Puerto Rico, 5
punch (n), 154
purple, 84
put, 6

quality, 44
question (n), 6
quick, 69
quickly, 69
quiet (adj), 76

Rachel, 142
radio (n), 65
Ralph, 154
Ramón, 9
read, 57
real, 2
red, 84
relax, 101
repeat (v), 75
report (n), 72
request (n), 76
respond, 30
restaurant, 96
rice, 107
Richard, 72
right (adj), 7
right now, 60
Rio de Janeiro, 9

(Isabel) Rivera, 118
Robert, 11
Roger, 142
Rome, 19
room, 48
Rosa, 2
Rose, 7
Roy, 20

sad, 7
salesman, 2
saleswoman, 5
Salvador, 9
same, 53
Sandra, 57
sandwich (n), 79
San Francisco, 9
San Juan, 19
Santiago, 9
Santo Domingo, 19
Sao Paulo, 9
Saturday, 102
school, 22
science, 53
scientist, 5
sculpture, 137
second (adj), 78
secretary, 3
see, 71
send, 93
sentence, 2
seven, 128
seventeen, 128
shark, 136
she, 1
sheep, 26
ship (n), 12
shirt, 86
shoe, 86
shop (n), 120
short, 6

show (n), 72
show (v), 137
sick, 6
simple, 110
sing, 58
singer, 66
singular, 16
sip (v), 73
sister, 14
sit, 77
six, 128
sixteen, 128
skirt (n), 152
sky, 46
sleep (v), 62
slow, 69
slowly, 69
small, 46
so (adv), 73
soccer, 92
soda, 106
son, 154
song, 53
(be) sorry, 74
sound (n), 100
soup, 73
souvenir, 120
Spain, 19
Spanish, 67
speak, 66
specified, 46
spelling (n), 101
sport (n), 120
sports stadium, 120
stadium, 120
stand (v), 78
state (n), 44
statement, 4
station (n), 121
statue, 138
stay (v), 72

(Barbara) Stern, 27
          stop (v), 73
          store (n), 98
          story, 52
          strawberry, 85
          stress (v), 128
          student, 1
          study (v), 59
          subject (n), 92
          subway, 121
          sugar (n), 107
 (Philip) Sullivan, 13
          Sunday, 102
          Surinam, 9
          Susan, 55
          swim (v), 102
          syllable, 128
          Sylvia, 24

          table, 72
          tail, 145
          talk (v), 59
          tall, 6
          taxi (n), 69
(George) Taylor, 57
          tea, 107
          teach, 97
          teacher, 5
          team (n), 92
          teeth, 119
          telephone (v), 102
          television, 58
          tell, 56
          ten, 128
          tennis, 67
          tense (gram), 97
          thanks, 55
          thank you, 38
          that (pron), 120
          the, 2
          theater, 70

          their, 138
          them, 79
          then, 77
          there, 69
          there are, 129
          there is, 129
          there's, 129
          these, 101
          they, 15
          thing, 90
          think, 60
          third, 97
          third person, 97
          thirsty, 29
          thirteen, 128
          this (adj), 11
          this (pron), 1
  (Mr.) Thompson, 137
          those, 120
          three, 128
          Thursday, 102
          time (n), 60
          tip (n), 105
          title (n), 138
          to, 7
          today, 27
          toe, 125
          together, 93
          Tom, 141
          tomato, 85
          tonight, 74
          too, 118
          tooth, 127
          Toshi, 2
          tourist, 1
          town, 136
          translator, 94
          travel (n), 25
          travel agent, 25
          Tuesday, 102
          twelve, 128

twenty, 128
twenty-five, 154
two, 80

ugly, 15
understand, 100
unhappy, 25
unique, 46
United Nations, 94
United States, 4
upper, 105
Uruguay, 9
us, 78
use (n), 69
use (v), 4

Venezuela, 5
Venezuelan, 5
verb, 4
very, 72
Victor, 2
Vincent, 12
Virginia, 112
visit (v), 79
visitor, 103
vowel, 49

wait (v), 74
waiter, 96
waitress, 149
wall, 130
want (v), 71
wash (v), 72
Washington (city), 9
Washington (state), 45
Washington, D.C., 131
watch (n), 21
watch (v), 58
water (n), 112
way, 104
we, 13

wear (v), 86
Wednesday, 102
week, 99
well (adj), 44
well (adv), 69
West Germany, 19
what, 43
when, 102
where, 38
white, 85
who, 43
(Linda) Wilson, 11
wine, 109
with, 6
without, 81
woman, 20
women, 127
word, 6
work (n), 101
work (v), 59
worker, 53
write, 58
wrong, 7

year, 60
yellow, 84
yes, 6
Yoko, 2
you, 13
young, 7
your, 13

zip, 56
zipper, 93

Index

adjective
  modifier of noun, 52
  possessive, 142
adverb
  with *how* questions, 69
answers
  short with *be,* 29
  short in the present progressive, 66
  short in the present tense (with *do,
    does, don't, doesn't*), 114
  short with *there is/there are,* 132
article
  a and *the,* 46
  a and *an,* 49
  omission of *a* in plural, 50
  with singular and plural nouns, 50
be
  am, are, is, 15
colors, 84
contractions
  of *be* 4, 17
  there's, 129
  isn't and *aren't,* 135
days of the week, 102
demonstratives, 122
how
  in questions with *be,* 43
  in questions with the present
    progressive, 68
intonation
  borders, 158
  levels, 158
  marks and stress, 158
modifiers of nouns, 52
negative
  requests, 76

statements with *be,* 31
short answers with *be,* 33
short answers in the present tense
  (with *don't, doesn't*), 114
short answers to yes/no questions in
  the present progressive, 66
statements in the present
  progressive, 63
statements in the present tense
  (with *don't, doesn't*), 108
noun(s)
  regular plural of, 21
  modifier of, 52
  possessive of, 145
numbers
  1 to 20, 128
objects
  verbs with two, 80
parts of the body, 125
plurals of nouns
  regular, 21
  irregular, 127
possessive
  adjectives, 142
  of nouns, 145
  pronunciation of, 148
pronouns
  subject, 17
  object, 78
  demonstrative, 122,
  possessive, 142
pronunciation
  see sounds
questions
  yes/no with *is,* 6
  yes/no with *be,* 22

yes/no in the present progressive, 65
yes/no in the present tense, (with
  do, does), 110
information with *be* (*who, what,
  where, how*), 43
information with the present
  progressive (*what, where, how*),
  68
about colors (*what color*), 89
with *there is/there are*, 131
subject with *who, what*, 150

requests
  affirmative and negative, 76
  polite, 77

short answers
  see answers

sounds
  [i] *ship*, 12
  [iy] *sheep*, 26
  [i] : [iy], 36
  [z] *zip*, 56
  [s] *sip*, 73
  [z] : [s], 93
  [d] *day*, 105
  [ð] *they*, 119
  [d] : [ð], 138
  [č] *chin*, 155
  possessive of nouns, 148
  third person singular of present
    tense, 100

statements
  affirmative with *be*, 4, 15
  affirmative with the present
    progressive, 60
  negative with *be*, 33

negative in the present progressive,
  63
negative in the present tense (with
  don't, doesn't), 108

there is/there are, 129

third person singular of present tense
  pronunciation of, 100
  -*s* ending, 97

this, that, these, those, 122

verb(s)
  with two objects, 80
  be, 15
  present progressive form, 60
  regular present tense, 97
  third person singular of present
    tense, 97
  pronunciation of third person
    singular of present tense, 100

week
  days of, 102

what
  in questions with *be*, 43
  in questions with the present
    progressive, 68
  in subject questions, 150

where
  in questions with *be*, 43
  in questions with the present
    progressive, 68

who
  in questions with *be*, 43
  in subject questions, 150

Notes

Notes

Notes

Notes